PAPERBACK SONGS

SOUL HITS

MELODY LINE, CHORDS AND LYRICS
FOR KEYBOARD • GUITAR • VOCAL

ISBN 0-634-03352-2

Printed in Canada

Visit Hal Leonard Online at
www.halleonard.com

Welcome to the PAPERBACK SONGS SERIES.

Do you play piano, guitar, electronic keyboard, sing or play any instrument for that matter? If so, this handy "pocket tune" book is for you.

The concise, one-line music notation consists of:

MELODY, LYRICS & CHORD SYMBOLS

Whether strumming the chords on guitar, "faking" an arrangement on piano/keyboard or singing the lyrics, these fake book style arrangements can be enjoyed at any experience level – hobbyist to professional.

The musical skills necessary to successfully use this book are minimal. If you play guitar and need some help with chords, a basic chord chart is included at the back of the book.

While playing and singing is the first thing that comes to mind when using this book, it can also serve as a compact, comprehensive reference guide.

However you choose to use this PAPERBACK SONGS SERIES book, by all means have fun!

CONTENTS

(contents continued)

(contents continued)

A BIT OF SOUL

Words and Music by
RAY CHARLES

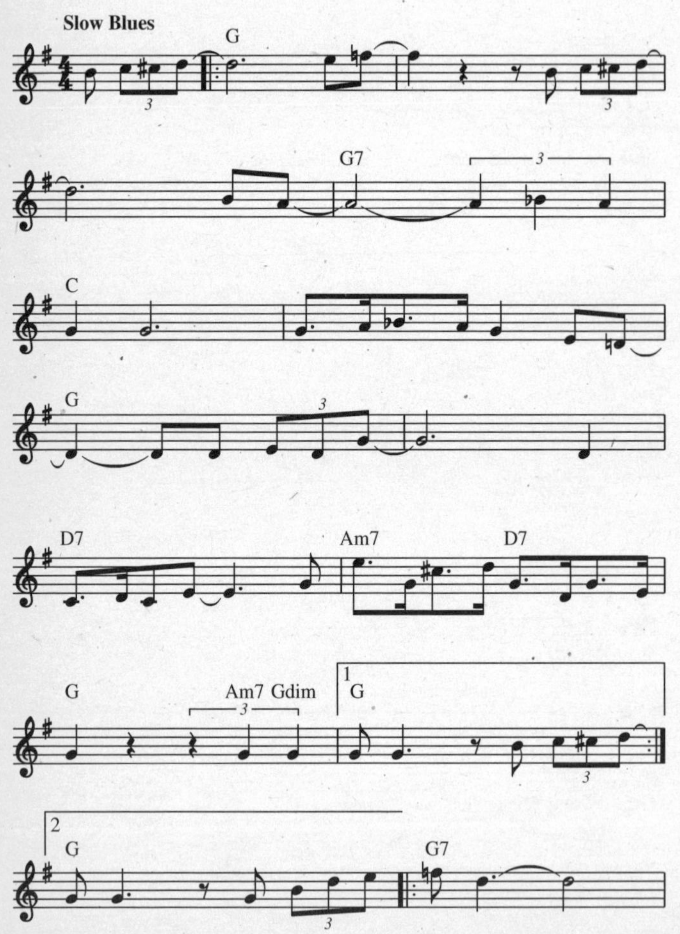

C7
G7
C7
G
D7
C7
1
G
2
G
G♯7 G7

BOOM BOOM

(Out Go the Lights)

Words and Music by
STAN LEWIS

C6
(Shake it, ba - by)
shake, shake it up,
(Shake it, ba - by)
ba - by. Come on, now,
F7
(Shake it, ba - by)
ba - by, I don't mean
C
(Shake it, ba - by)
may - be. You're driv - in' me
Come on, come
G7
F7
(Shake it, ba - by)
cra - zy. Come on, come on.
on. All right, all right.
1
C
(Shake it, ba - by)
Come on and
2
C
(Shake it, ba - by)

BORN UNDER A BAD SIGN

Words and Music by BOOKER T. JONES
and WILLIAM BELL

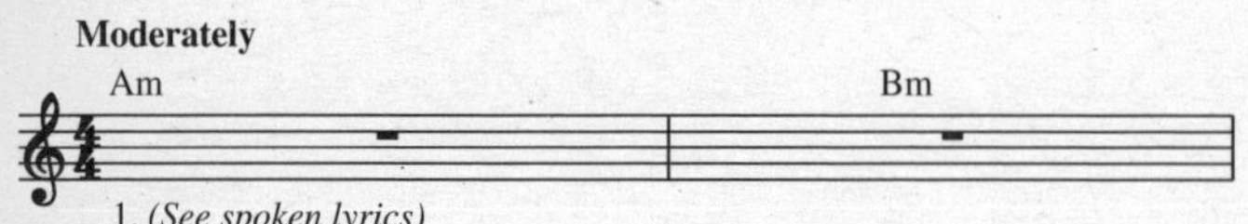
Moderately
Am
Bm
1. (See spoken lyrics)

Am
Bm
Repeat as needed

Am
Born un - der a bad sign;

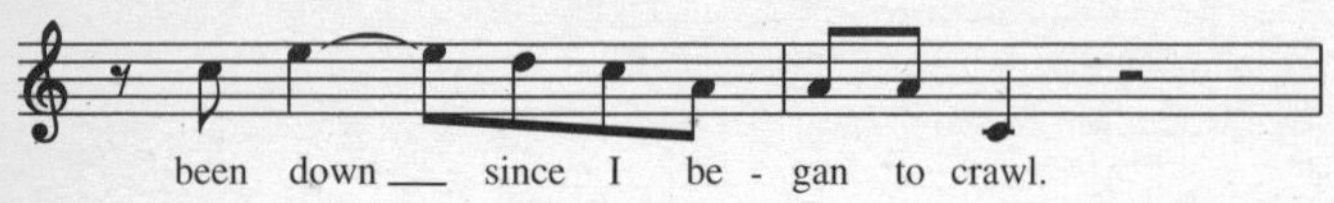
been down since I be - gan to crawl.

E
Oh, if it was - n't for bad

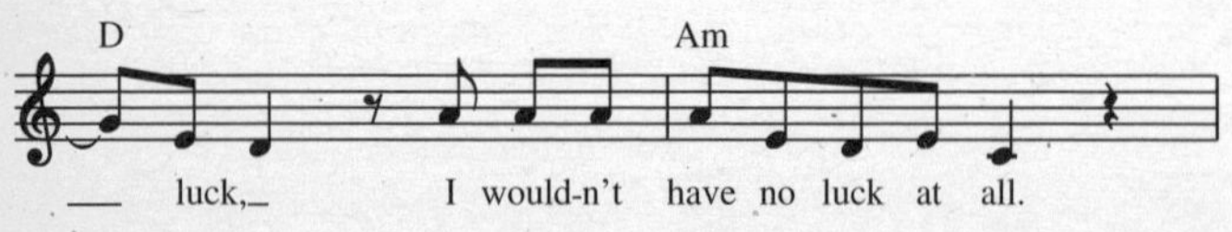
D
Am
luck, I would-n't have no luck at all.

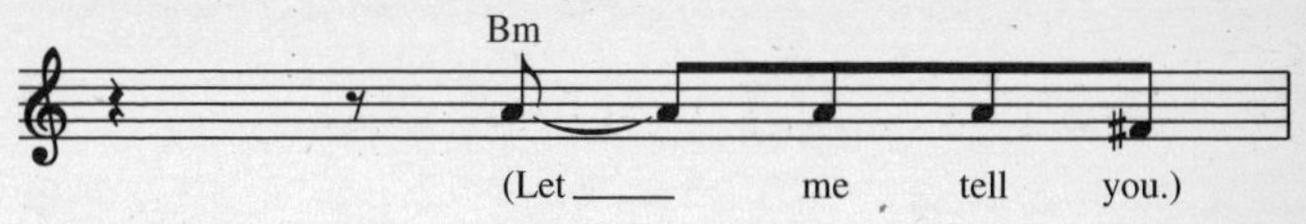
Bm
(Let me tell you.)

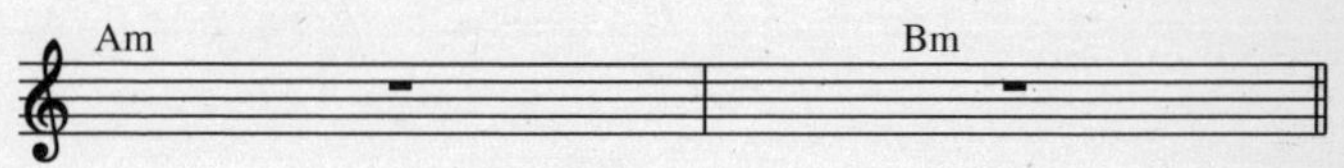
Am
Bm

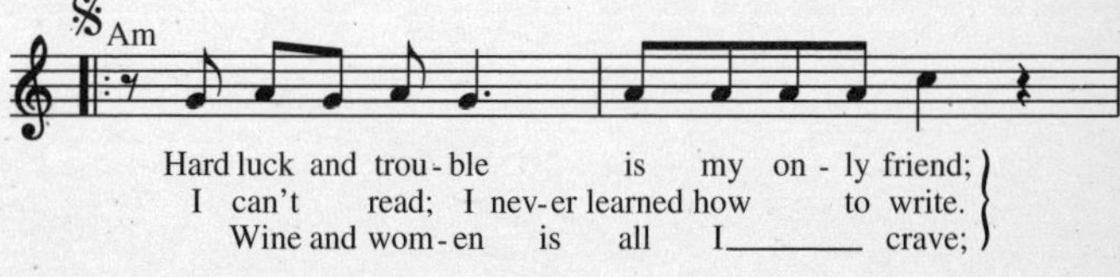
Am
Hard luck and trou - ble is my on - ly friend;
I can't read; I nev-er learned how to write.
Wine and wom-en is all I crave;

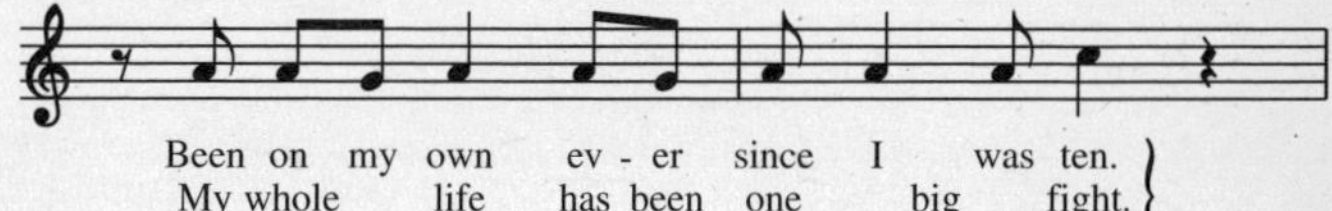
Been on my own ev - er since I was ten.
My whole life has been one big fight.
A big head wom-an will car-ry me to my grave.

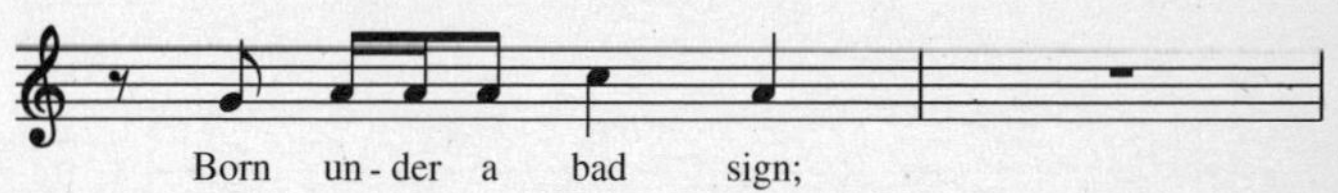
Born un-der a bad sign;

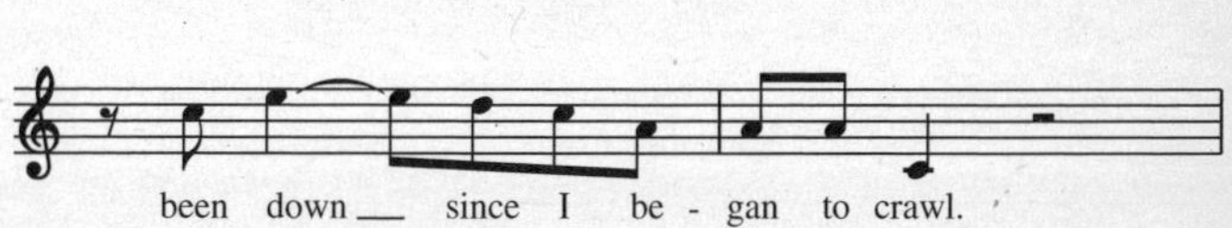
been down since I be - gan to crawl.

E
Oh, if it was - n't for bad

D
Am
— luck, _ I would-n't have no luck at all.
Bm
Am
To Coda
Bm
Am
2. (See spoken lyrics)
Bm
Am
Repeat ad lib.
Bm
Last time
N.C.
D.S. al Coda
CODA
Repeat and Fade
Am
Bm

(Spoken ad lib.)
I'm gonna get myself together now, I'm gonna keep on pushing.

Spoken Lyrics

1. When I was just a little boy, my daddy left home.
   He left me and my mama to go it all alone.
   You know, the times were hard, but somehow we survived.
   Lord knows, it's a mystery to me how she managed to keep us alive.

2. I've often heard the old folks say,
   "Don't give up, when the chips are down, you got to keep on pushing."
   So I guess I gotta keep on pushing.
   You see, I was down, but I kind of picked myself up a little bit,
   Oh, and I had to dust myself off, clean myself up,
   And now, I'm gonna keep on pushing; I can't stop.

CHAINS OF LOVE

Words and Music by A. NUGETRE
and HARRY VANWALLS

E♭7
Are you gon - na leave me,
are you gon - na make me cry?
B♭
F7♯9
These chains are gon - na haunt me
un - til the day I die.
B♭
Well, if you're gon - na leave me,
E♭7
please, won't you set me free?
B♭
E♭7
Well, if you're gon - na leave me,
please, won't you set me free?
B♭

F7
I can't bear these chains that bind me
un - less you're here with me.
Bb
Well, it's three o'-clock in the morn - in',
Eb7
the moon is shin - in' bright.
Bb
Eb7
Yes, it's three o'-clock in the morn - in',
the moon is shin - in' bright.
Bb
F7#9
I just sit and won-der: Where can you be to -
1
Bb
Cm
F7
night?
2
Bb
night?
3

CAN'T GET ENOUGH OF YOUR LOVE, BABE

Words and Music by
BARRY WHITE

B♭maj7 Am7 Gm7 Gm7/C
no mat - ter how I try.
and make you un - der - stand.
F Am7 Dm7 B♭maj7 Am7 Gm7 Gm7/C
It seems the more
Boy, your love
F Am7 Dm7
you give the more I want
for me is all I need now,
B♭maj7 Am7 Gm7 Gm7/C
and, ba - by, that's no lie.
and more than I can stand.
F Am7 Dm7 B♭maj7 Am7 Gm7 Gm7/C
Oh, no. Tell me.
Oh, well.
B♭maj7
What can I say, what am I gon - na do?
How can I ex-plain all the things I feel?
Am7
How should I feel when
You've giv - en me so much.

Dm7
ev - 'ry - thing __ is you, you, __ you?
Boy, it's so un - real, un - real, un - real.
B♭maj7
What kind of a love __ is this
Well, I ___ keep lov - in' ___ you
that you're giv - ing me? ______
more and more _ each time. ______
Am7
Is it in ___ your kiss or
Boy, what am I gon - na do
Dm7
just be - cause _ you're sweet, ___ sweet? __
'cause you' blow __ my mind, ___ mind. __
B♭maj7
You're all I ___ know __
I got the same old __ feel -
and ev - 'ry time you're _ near
ing ev - 'ry time you're _ near.

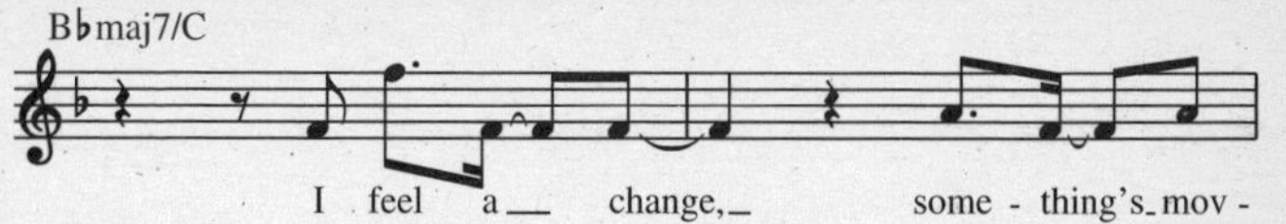
B♭maj7/C
I feel a change, some - thing's mov -

ing, I scream your name. What ya got me do - ing?

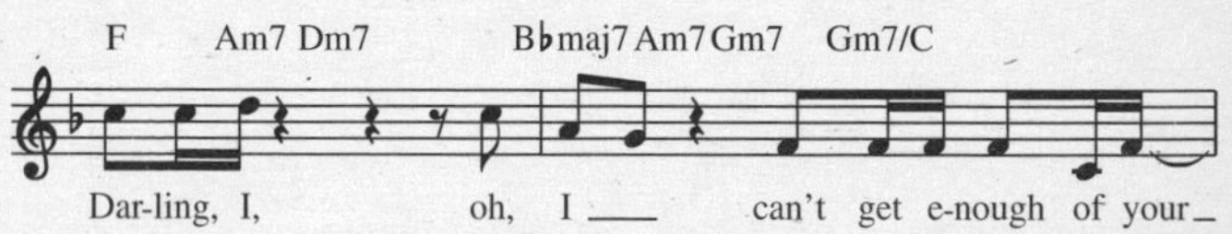
F Am7 Dm7 B♭maj7 Am7 Gm7 Gm7/C
Dar-ling, I, oh, I can't get e-nough of your

F Am7 Dm7 B♭maj7 Am7 Gm7 Gm7/C
love, ba - by. Oh.

B♭maj7
Ba - by, it did - n't take

Am7
all of my life to find you and it sure

Fmaj7 Gm7 Am7
ain't gon - na take the rest of my life to

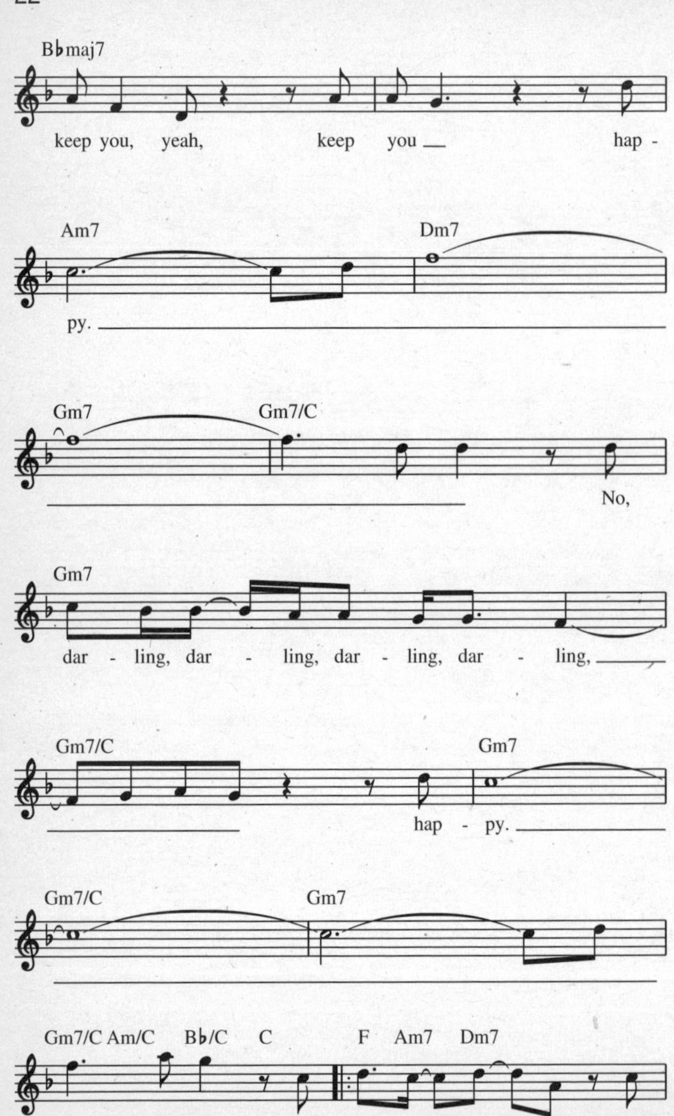
B♭maj7
keep you, yeah, keep you __ hap -
Am7
Dm7
py. ____
Gm7
Gm7/C
____ No,
Gm7
dar - ling, dar - ling, dar - ling, dar - ling, ____
Gm7/C
Gm7
____ hap - py. ____
Gm7/C
Gm7
____
Gm7/C Am/C B♭/C C
F Am7 Dm7
__ oo. __ My dar - ling, _ I, ____ oh,

B♭maj7 Am7 Gm7 Gm7/C
I ___ can't get e - nough of your _
F Am7 Dm7 B♭maj7 Am7 Gm7 Gm7/C
_ love, ba - by. Woo, _ I
F Am7 Dm7
don't know, _ I don't know, I don't know
B♭maj7 Am7 Gm7 Gm7/C F Am7 Dm7
why I can't get e-nough of your _ love, ba - by.
B♭maj7 Am7 Gm7 Gm7/C F Am7 Dm7
Oh, _ my _ _ love, your love, your love, _
B♭maj7 Am7 Gm7 Gm7/C F Am7 Dm7
___ woo, _ hoo. Can't get e-nough, can't get e-nough,
Repeat and Fade
B♭maj7 Am7 Gm7 Gm7/C
can't get e - nough, can't get e - nough.

COLD SWEAT, PT. 1

Words and Music by JAMES BROWN
and ALFRED JAMES ELLIS

C7
F7
fy your thoughts,
stand me al - ways.
C7
F7
When you kiss me,
C7
F7
when you miss me,
C7
F7
hold my hand,
C7
make me un - der - stand.
F7
N.C.
I wake up
in a cold sweat!
1
G9
2
G9
I don't

COME BACK BABY

Words and Music by
RAY CHARLES

E9
B7#5
by,
oh, that I
a like a moun -
Guitar solo
E9
was wrong,
Don't you know, ba -
tain jack,
I'd go up on the moun-
A7
A9
G9
- by?
Child, you been gone
- tain;
peo - ple, I'd call my
F#9
A
A#dim7
too long.
Oh,
come back,
ba-by back.
Oh,
come back,
E/B
C#m
ba - by.
Yeah, yeah,
ba - by.
Oo.
Yeah,
F#7
B7#5
let's talk it o - ver
a one more
yeah.
Let's talk it o - ver
a one more
E7
A7
time.
Oh, now,
time.
Oh, now,
1
E7
B7#5
yeah.
I said, if I could hol - ler.

2
E7
B7♯5
3
E7
B7♯5
now.
E
B7♯5
Now, one of these days ba - by,
E
N.C.
and it won't be long, yeah,
A7
N.C.
G7
you're gon-na look for me, child, you know,
F♯7
A
A♯dim7
and I'll be gone. So come back,
E/B
C♯m
ba - a - a - by. Yeah,
F♯7
B7♯5
yeah, let's talk it o - ver a one more
E7
A7
E
time. Oh, now, now.

DO RIGHT WOMAN DO RIGHT MAN

Words and Music by DAN PENN and CHIPS MOMAN

A
Bm/E
and temp - ta - tion strong.
A
B7
A wom-an's on - ly
E/F#
B7
hu - man;
you should un - der -
B6/D# F#m E7
E7sus
stand.
She's not just a play
E7
E7sus
E7
E7sus
- thing;
she's flesh and blood,
just like her
E7
Bm/A
A/E
D6
A/C#
man.
If you want a do right, all day's
B7
E/F#
B7
wom-an,
you've got - ta be a
Dmaj7/E
E7
Dmaj7/E
E7
do right, all right

To Coda
1
To next strain
A
Bm/E
A
man.
Yeah,
2
D.S.S. al Coda
A
A7 B♭7
F♯m
yeah.
Well, they say it's a
C♯m
man's world;
oh, but you can't prove that by
F♯m
me,
no.
And as long as we're to -
B6/F♯ F♯m D/E
geth-er, ba-by,
show some re - spect for
D.S.
(Take 2nd ending)
CODA
E7
N.C.
A
me.
If you want a
You got-ta be a
Dmaj7/E
E7
Dmaj7/E
E7
do
right,
all
night
A
Bm
A
man.

DO THE FUNKY CHICKEN

Words and Music by
RUFUS THOMAS

Moderately fast

E7#9
You put your left arm up, right arm too. Let
both arms up a - bove your face and your
work both arms and you work both feet We to -

me tell you what you've got to do.
knees start wig - glin' all o - ver the place
geth - er, ba - by. You right on the beat.

Flap your wings and your feet start kick-in'.

Then you know you're doin' the funk-y chick-en.

(Instrumental)

(Come on and do the funk - y chick-en.)

(Instrumental)

To Coda
(Come on and do the funk - y chick-en.)

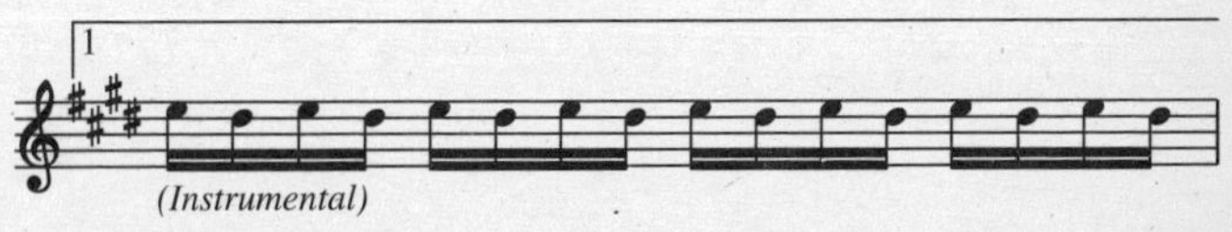
1
(Instrumental)

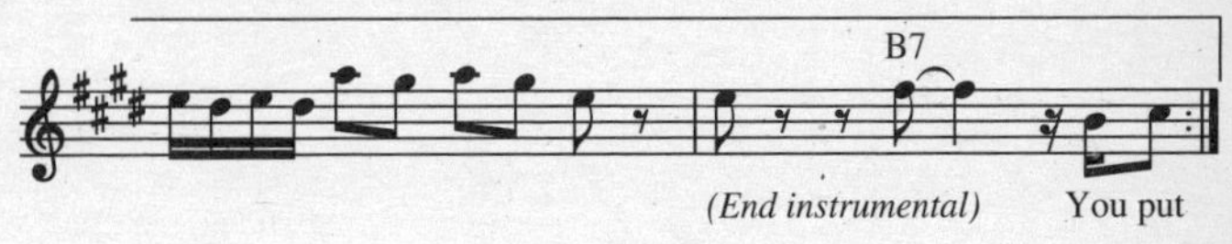
B7
(End instrumental)
You put

2
(Instrumental)

(Come on and do the funk - y chick-en.)

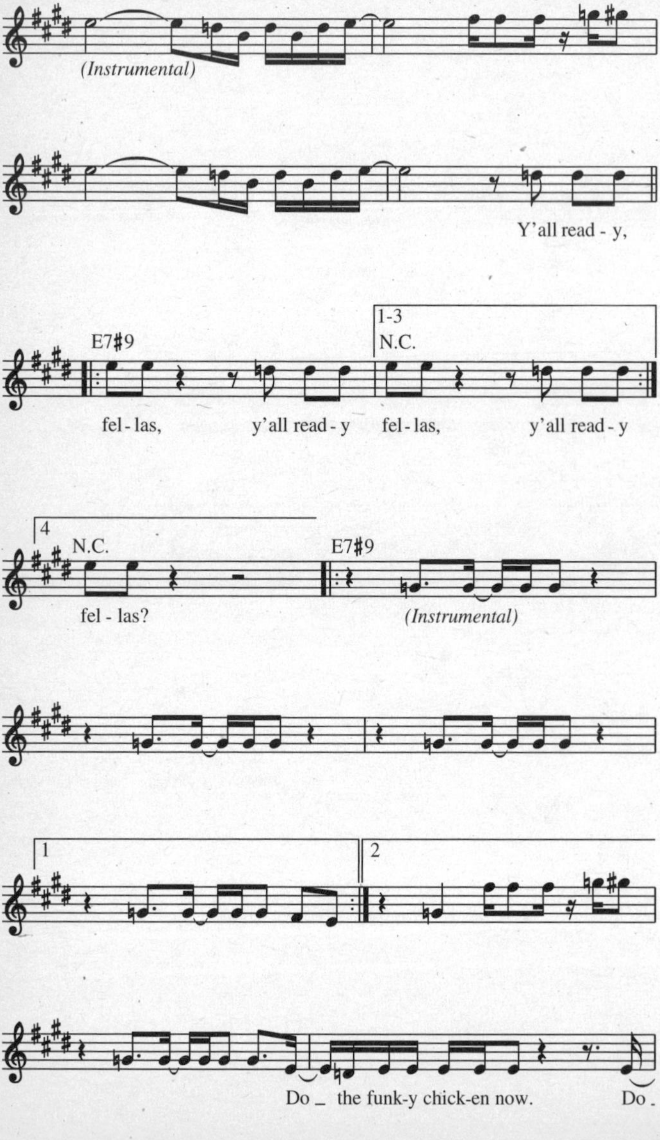

(Instrumental)

Y'all read - y,

E7#9

1-3

N.C.

fel - las, y'all read - y fel - las, y'all read - y

4

N.C.

E7#9

fel - las?

(Instrumental)

1

2

Do _ the funk-y chick-en now.
Do _

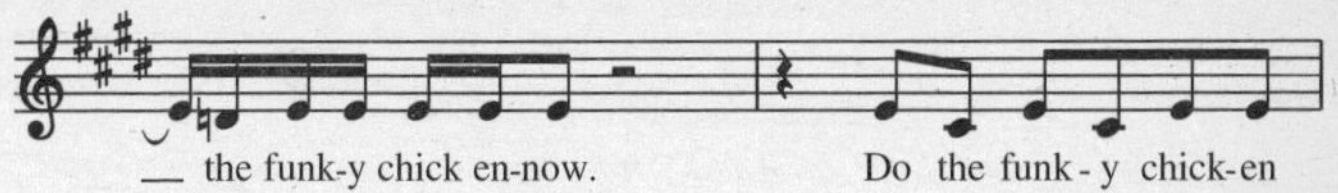

— the funk-y chick en-now.
Do the funk - y chick-en

now
all o - ver the place.
(Instrumental)

D.S. al Coda
N.C.
E7
B7
(End instrumental)
You

CODA
E7#9
Do the funk - y chick-en now.
Do

the funk - y chick - en now.
Do

Repeat and Fade
the funk-y chick-en now.
Do the funk-y chick-en now.

DO YOUR THING

Words and Music by
ISAAC HAYES

Moderately slow
Fm7
If the mu - sic makes you move, 'cause
feel like you wan - na scream, 'cause
you can dig the groove, then groove on, groove
that's your way of let-tin' off steam, scream on, scream
on.
on.
If you feel like you wan-na make love
If you feel like you wan-na sing, 'cause
un-der the stars a - bove, love on, love
sing - in' is your thing, sing on, sing
on,
on.
If it's some-thin' you wan-na say and
If you wan - na make love all night,
talk - in' is the on - ly way, rap
and you feel it's right, right

on,
oh, rap on.
on,
right on.
'Cause what ev -
Ab
C7
- er,
oh, you do,
oh, you got to do your
1
Fm7
thing, yeah.
If you
2
Fm7
thing now.
Do your thing.
(Instrumental)
Fm7
Repeat ad lib. and Fade

A FOOL FOR YOU

Words and Music by
RAY CHARLES

Slowly
E♭
I know you told me such a long time a -
E♭7
go, that you did - n't want me,
A♭7
you did-n't want me no
E♭
more. I wan - na know, oh, what makes me
F7
be? Do you be-lieve me child?
B♭7
I'm a fool for
E♭
you.
A♭
Oh, oh, Lord, I'm a fool for you.
E♭
B♭+
I know you
E♭
told me you did-n't want me a - round.
E♭7
Yeah and I
A♭7
know you got a man 'way a - cross

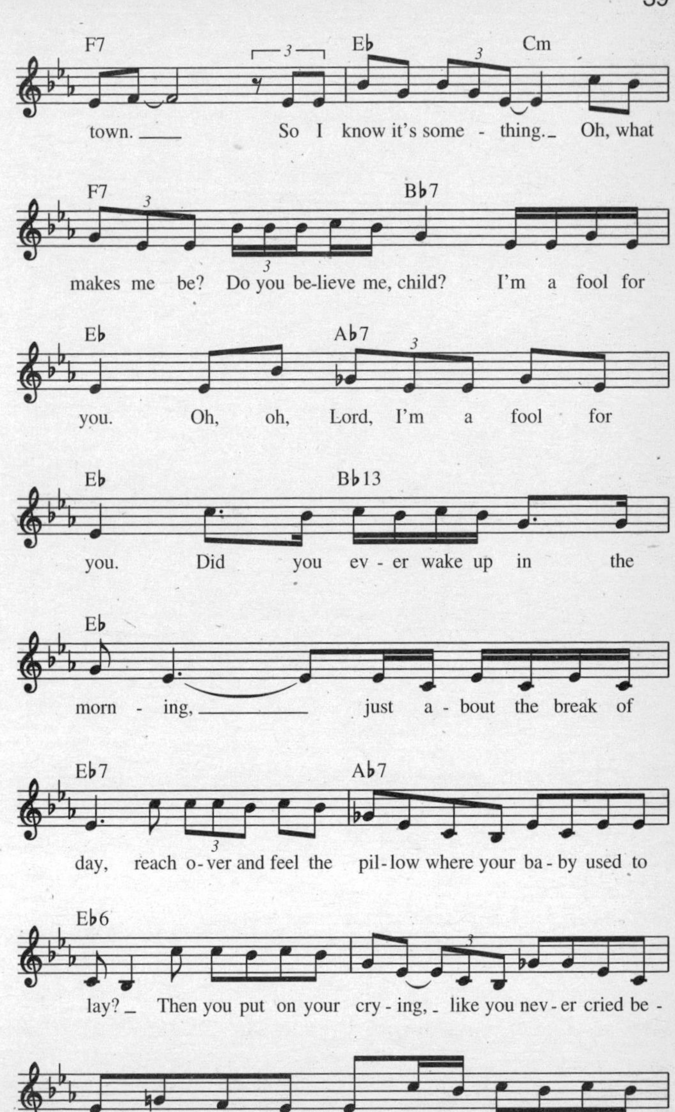
F7
Eb
Cm
town. So I know it's some - thing. Oh, what
F7
Bb7
makes me be? Do you be-lieve me, child? I'm a fool for
Eb
Ab7
you. Oh, oh, Lord, I'm a fool for
Eb
Bb13
you. Did you ev - er wake up in the
Eb
morn - ing, just a - bout the break of
Eb7
Ab7
day, reach o-ver and feel the pil-low where your ba-by used to
Eb6
lay? Then you put on your cry-ing, like you nev-er cried be -
fore. Oh, Lord, yes, you'll e - ven cry so

loud, you'll give the blues to your neigh - bor next
Bb7#5
door. Ev - er since you were five years
Eb
old, baby, I've been a fool for you. Lit - tle
Eb7
girl, 'way down in my
Ab7
soul, I'm a lit - tle fool for
Eb
C7
you. So I know it's some - thing, yes.
F7
Bb7
Oh, Lord, I'm a fool for
Eb7
Ab7
Eb7
you.

GET UP
(I Feel Like Being)
A SEX MACHINE

Words and Music by JAMES BROWN,
BOBBY BYRD and RONALD LENHOFF

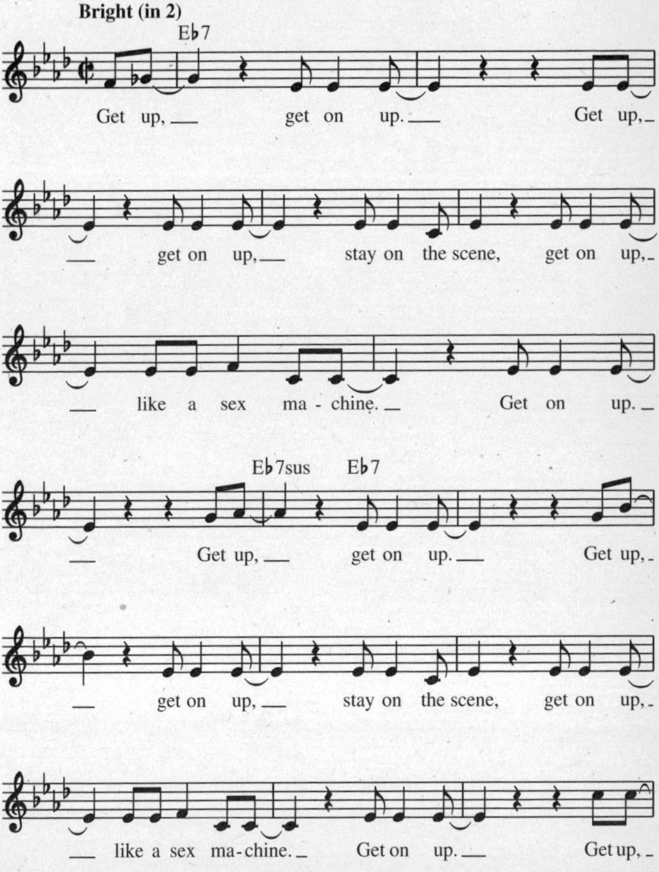

Bright (in 2)
E♭7
Get up, get on up. Get up,
get on up, stay on the scene, get on up,
like a sex ma-chine. Get on up.
E♭7sus
E♭7
Get up, get on up. Get up,
get on up, stay on the scene, get on up,
like a sex ma-chine. Get on up. Get up,

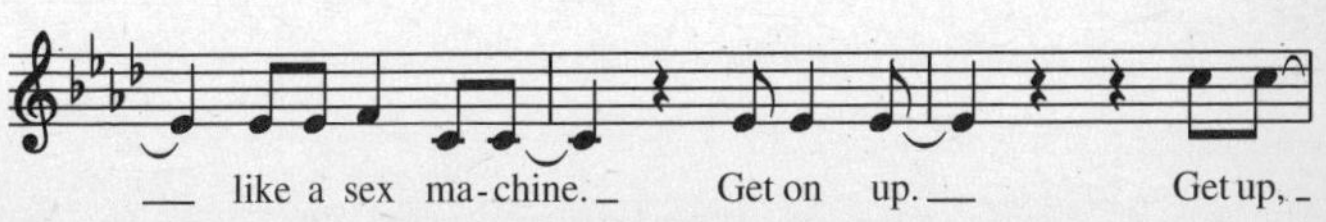

get on up, stay on the scene, get on up,

like a sex ma - chine. Get on up.

Wait a min-ute! Shake your arm

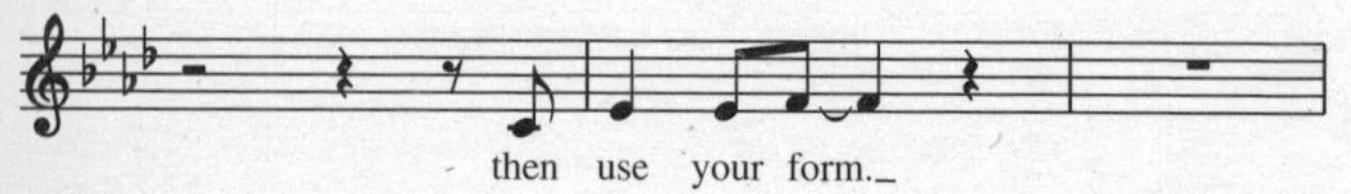
then use your form.

Stay on the scene like a sex ma-chine.

You got to have the feel - ing

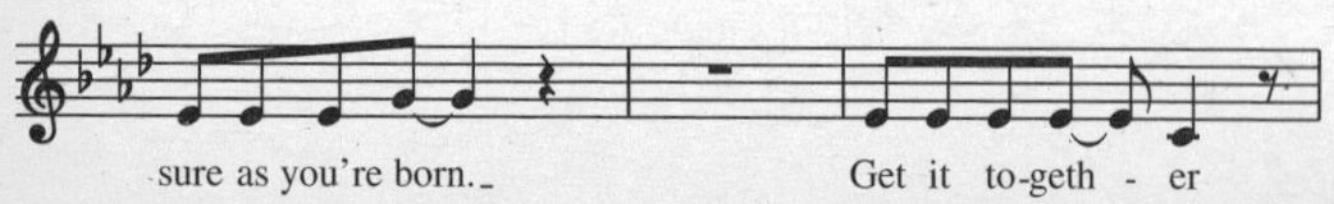
sure as you're born. Get it to-geth - er

right on, right on.
Get up,
get on up.
Get up,
Eb7
Eb7
get on up.
Get up,
get on up.
Eb7
(Instrumental and vocal ad lib.)
(See additional lyrics)
3
1, etc.
Last time
D.S. and Fade
Get up

Additional Lyrics

I said the feeling you got to get,
Give me the fever in a cold sweat.
The way I like it is the way it is;
I got mine and don't worry 'bout his.

Get on up and then shake your money maker,
Shake your money maker, etc.

GEE WHIZ

Words and Music by
CARLA THOMAS

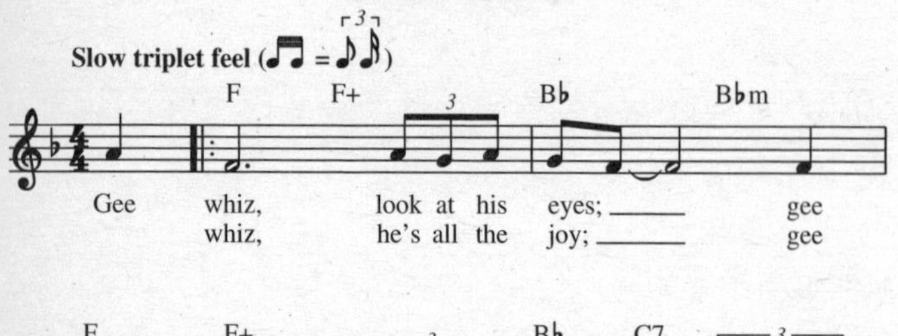

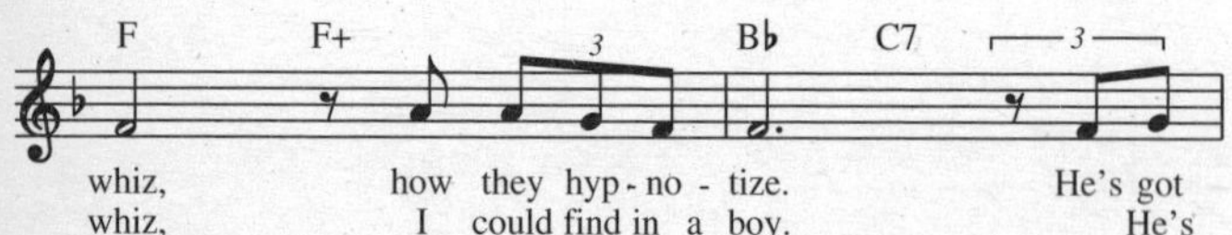

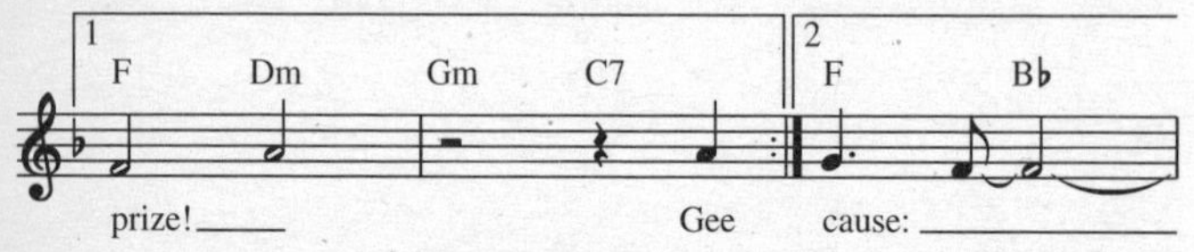

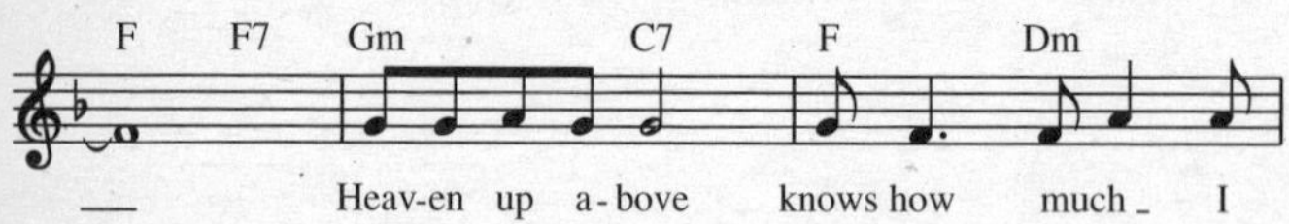

B♭ C7 F Dm

An - gels sing ___ of the love I ___ bring; I

G9 C7

hope our love will grow and grow. Oh, ___ gee

F F+ B♭ B♭m

whiz, I love that guy; gee

F F+ B♭ C7

whiz, my, my, oh my. There are

F Dm

things we could do, I could

F Dm B♭/F C7

say I love you; but all I could say is ___

GEORGIA ON MY MIND

Words by STUART GORRELL
Music by HOAGY CARMICHAEL

Dm Gm6 Dm B♭7
Oth - er arms reach out to me;
Dm Gm6 Dm7 G7
Oth - er eyes smile ten - der - ly;
Dm Gm6 Dm7 E7
Still in peace - ful dreams I see the
Am F♯dim7 Am C7 F
road leads back to you, Geor - gia,
A7 Dm Gm B♭m
Geor - gia, no peace I find, Just an
F Gm G9 C13 1 F Dm
old sweet song keeps Geor - gia on my mind.
Gm7 C13 2 F B♭13 F6
mind.

GREEN ONIONS

Written by AL JACKSON, JR., LEWIS STEINBERG, BOOKER T. JONES and STEVE CROPPER

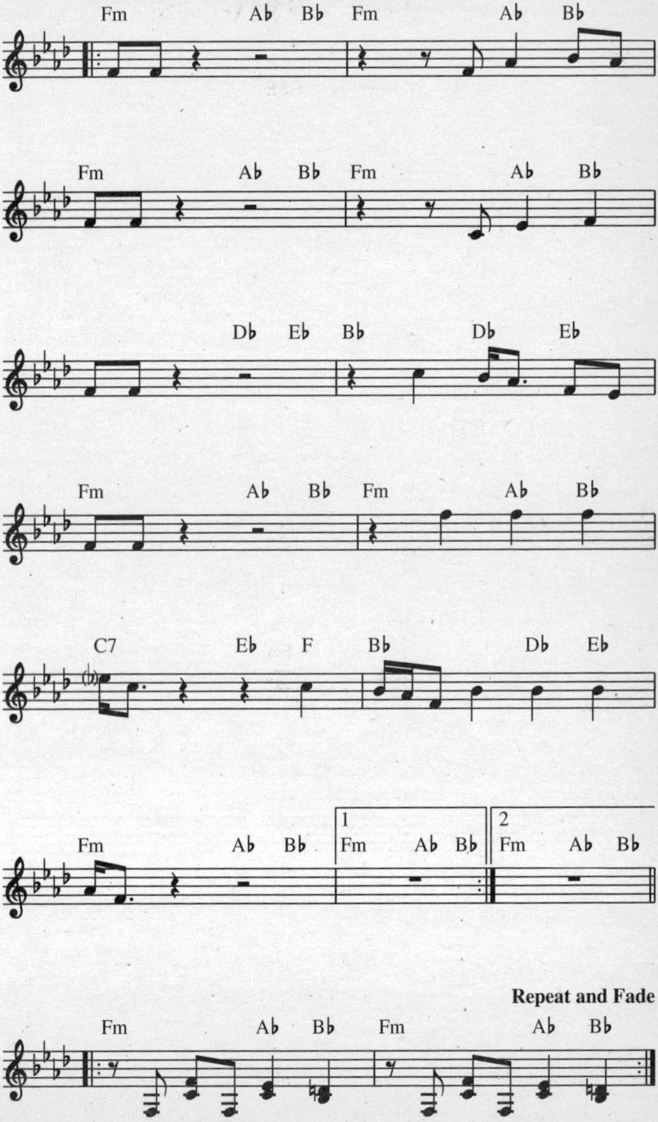

Fm Ab Bb Fm Ab Bb
Fm Ab Bb Fm Ab Bb
Db Eb Bb Db Eb
Fm Ab Bb Fm Ab Bb
C7 Eb F Bb Db Eb
1
2
Fm Ab Bb Fm Ab Bb Fm Ab Bb
Repeat and Fade
Fm Ab Bb Fm Ab Bb

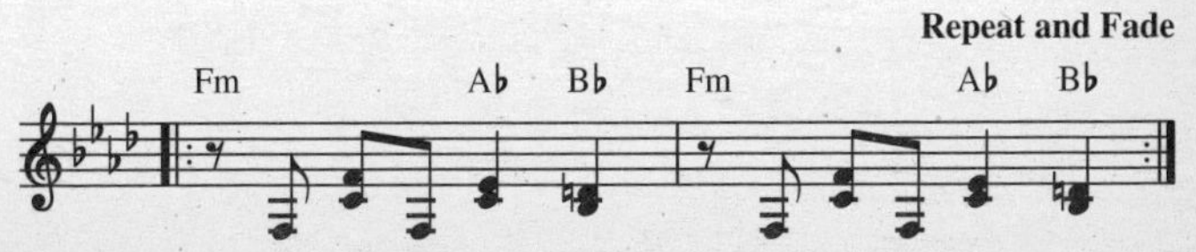

GROOVIN'

Words and Music by FELIX CAVALIERE
and EDWARD BRIGATI, JR.

B♭maj7 Cm7 F11
We'll keep on spend-in' sun - ny days this way.

B♭maj7 Cm7 F11
We're gon - na talk and laugh our time a - way.

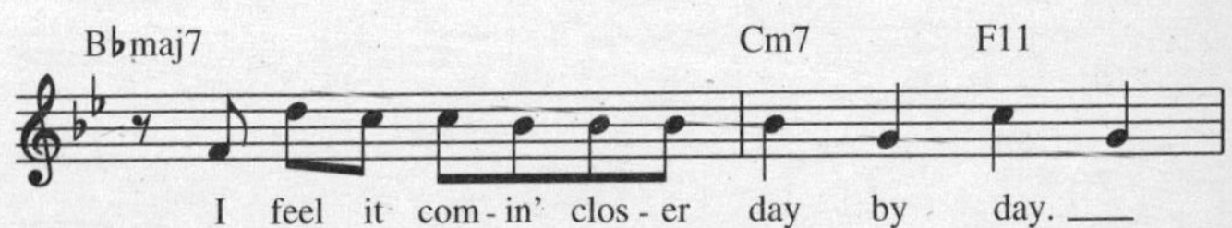
B♭maj7 Cm7 F11
I feel it com - in' clos - er day by day.

E♭ Dm Cm7 F11 B♭
Life would be ec - sta-sy you and me end - less-ly groov - in'

Cm7 F11 B♭ Cm7 F11
on a Sun-day af - ter - noon,

B♭ Cm7 F11 B♭
3
real - ly could-n't get a-way too soon, no, no, no,

Repeat and Fade

Cm7 F11 B♭ Cm7 F11
no. Groov - in' ah ha ah ha.

HALLELUJAH I LOVE HIM (HER) SO

Words and Music by
RAY CHARLES

Moderately
F
Bb
Bdim7
Let_ me tell you 'bout a boy I know._
(girl)
F
Bb
Bdim7 C7
He is my ba - by and he lives next door.
(She) (she)
F
F7
F7#5
Ev - 'ry morn - ing 'fore the sun comes up
Bb
Bdim7
He brings my cof - fee in my fav - 'rite cup._ That's why I
(She)
F
A7/E
Dm
Bb7
know,_ yes, I know,_ hal - le -
G7
C7sus
F
lu - jah, I just love him so.
(her)
Bb
Bdim7
F
Now if I call him on the tel - e-phone., And tell him that I'm
(her) (her)

F7
F7#5
Bb9
all a - lone,
by the time I count from
Ab9
G7
C7
one to four,
I hear him
(her)
on my door.
F
Bb
Bdim7
In the eve - ning when the sun goes down,
F
Bb
Bdim7
C7
when there is no-bod - y else a - round,
F
F7
F7#5
he kiss - es me and he holds me tight.
(she)
(she)
Bb
Bdim7
He tells me, "Ba - by ev - 'ry-thing's all right." That's why I
(She)
F
A7/E
Dm
Bb7
know, yes, I know, hal - le -
G7
C7sus
F
Bb7
F
lu - jah, I just love him so.
(her)

THE HAPPY SONG

Words and Music by OTIS REDDING
and STEVE CROPPER

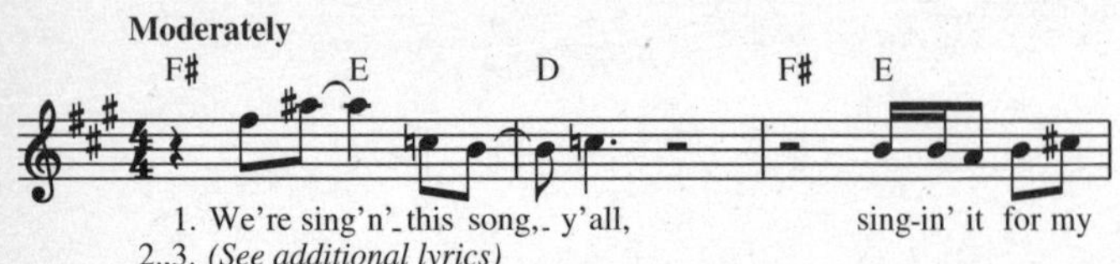
Moderately
F#
E
D
F#
E
1. We're sing'n' this song, y'all,
sing-in' it for my
2.,3. (See additional lyrics)

D
F#
E
D
ba - by.
She's the on - ly one can bring me joy;

Chorus:
A
that's why I sing these hap-py songs. They go:
Dum-dum, di-di -

To Coda
D
A
D
di, dum - dum,
dum-dum, di - di - di, dum - dum.

A
D
C/D D
Dum-dum, di-di - di, dum dum,_come on now.
Hap-py song,

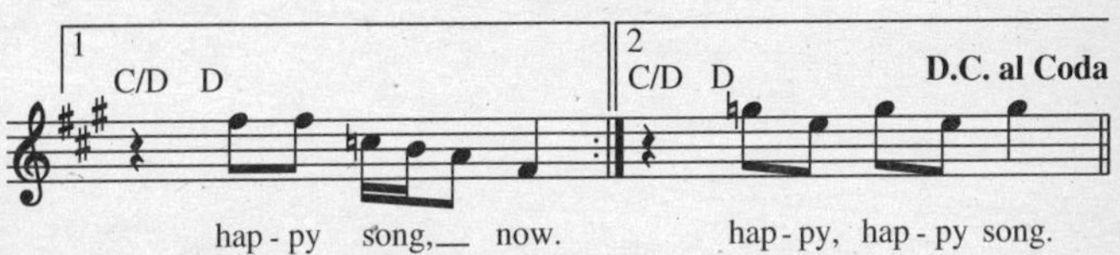
1
C/D D
2
C/D D
D.C. al Coda
hap - py song,__ now.
hap - py, hap - py song.

CODA
A
D7
Repeat and Fade
(Vocal ad lib.)

Additional Lyrics

2. On a cold, windy, rainy night,
She shut all my doors, she cut off the light.
She hold me and squeeze me tight,
She tell me: "Big O, everything's all right," and I go
To Chorus

3. Bring my breakfast to the table;
When I go to work she know I'm able.
Do my job, when I come back in,
You oughta' see my baby's face, she just grin, grin, grin.
To Chorus

HARD TO HANDLE

Words and Music by ALLEN JONES, ALVERTIS BELL and OTIS REDDING

Moderate Funk

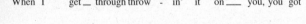

Bb7
1.,3. Ba - by, here I am I'm a man on the scene.
2. (See additional lyrics)

I can give you what you want, but you got to go home with me.

I've got some good old lov - in' and I've got some in store.

When I get through throw - in' it on you, you got

F7
to come back for more. Boys and things will come by the doz-en; but

that ain't noth - in' but drug - store lov - in'.
N.C.
Pret - ty lit - tle thing, let me light the can - dle,'cause
ma - ma I'm sure hard to han - dle now, yes I am.
1
Eb
F
Eb
Bb
(Instrumental)
2,3
Ab Eb
Bb
(Instrumental)
1
D.C.
(take 3rd ending)
2
Ab
Eb
Bb
Ab Eb
Bb

Additional Lyrics

2. Action speaks louder than words,
   and I'm a man with a great experience.
   I know you got you another man,
   but I can love you better than him.
   Take my hand, don't be afraid,
   I want to prove every word that I said.
   I'm advertising love for free,
   so won't you place your ad with me?
   Boys will come a dime by the dozen,
   but that ain't nothin' but kiss and look.
   Pretty little thing, let me light the candle,
   'cause mama, I'm sure hard to handle, now.

HOLD ON I'M COMIN'

Words and Music by ISAAC HAYES
and DAVID PORTER

Moderately, with a strong beat

G7

Don't you ev - er feel sad; ___ lean

C7

on me when times _ are bad. _ When the day ___ comes and you're

down _ in a riv-er of trou-ble and I got to drown, just hold

G Bb C **To Coda**

on, I'm com-in'. Hold on, ___ I'm

G G7

com-in'. I'm goin' my way, your lov-er. If

C7

you get cold _ I'll be your cov-er. Don't have to wor - ry 'cause I'm

here. No need to suf-fer, _ 'cause I'm here. 'Cause hold

G Bb C
on, I'm com-in'. Hold on, I'm
1 G 2 G C7
com-in'. Hold com-in'. (Look here.) Reach out to me
for sat - is - fac - tion, yeah.
Bb C
Call my name, now, for quick re - ac - tion, eh, eh, eh,
D7 G F Bb
yeah. (Instrumental)
D.C. al Coda
C
CODA
G G
com-in'.
(Instrumental
and vocal ad lib.)
Bb C
1 G 2 N.C.

I CAN'T GET NEXT TO YOU

Words and Music by BARRETT STRONG
and NORMAN WHITFIELD

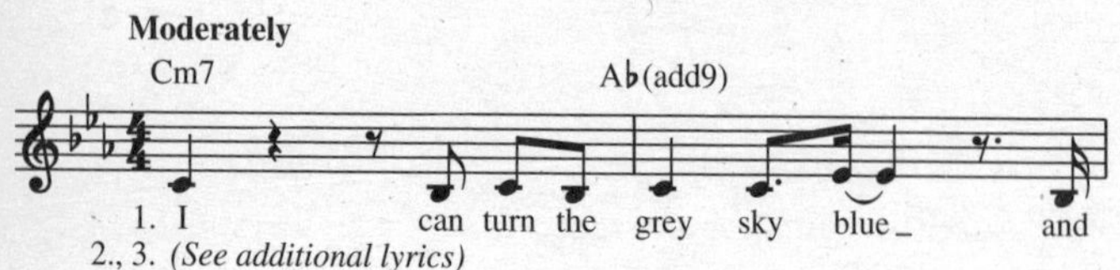
Moderately
Cm7
A♭(add9)
1. I can turn the grey sky blue and
2., 3. (See additional lyrics)

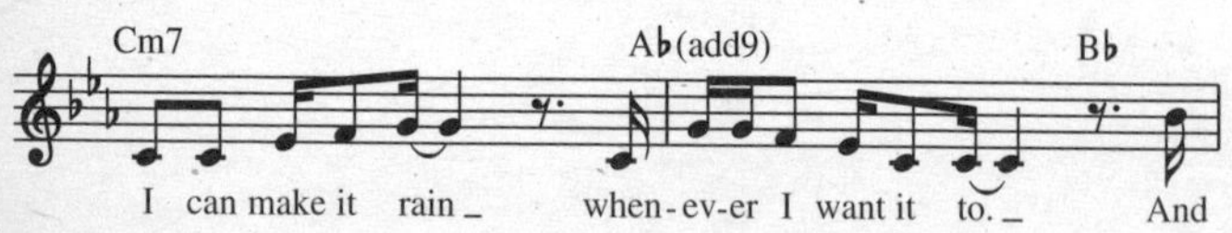
Cm7
A♭(add9)
B♭
I can make it rain when-ev-er I want it to. And

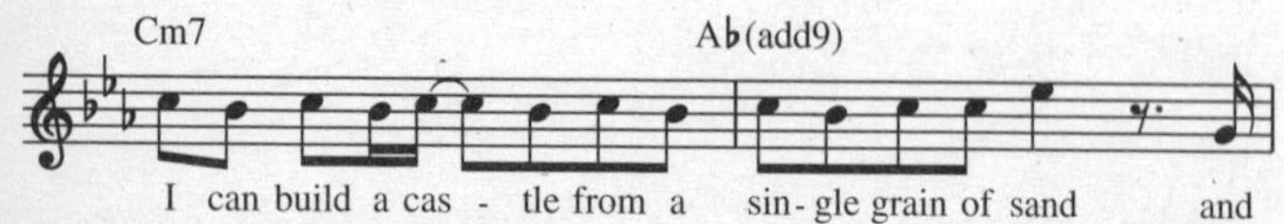
Cm7
A♭(add9)
I can build a cas - tle from a sin-gle grain of sand and

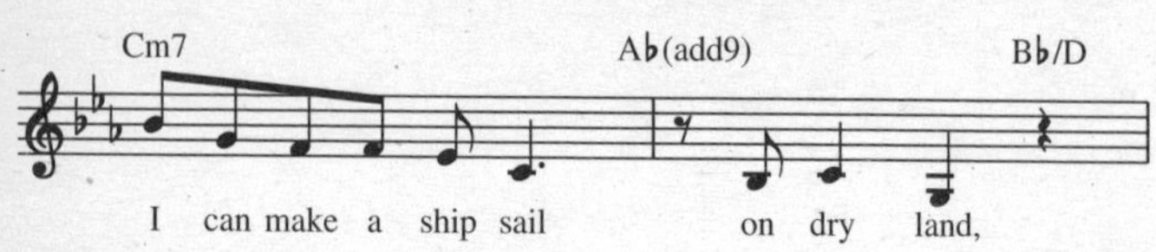
Cm7
A♭(add9)
B♭/D
I can make a ship sail on dry land,

Fm
Cm
To Coda
but my life is in-com-plete and I'm so blue. 'Cause

Fm
Cm
I can't get next to you
I can't get next to you babe, I

Fsus
Cm
can't get next to you, I can't get next to you babe, I
1
Fsus
Cm7
can't get next to you.
(Instrumental)
Ab(add9)
Cm7
Abadd9
Bb/D
2
Fsus
can't get next to you, I
Cm7
can't get next to you babe, I
Fsus
can't get next to you.
(Instrumental)
Cm7
Ab(add9)
Bb

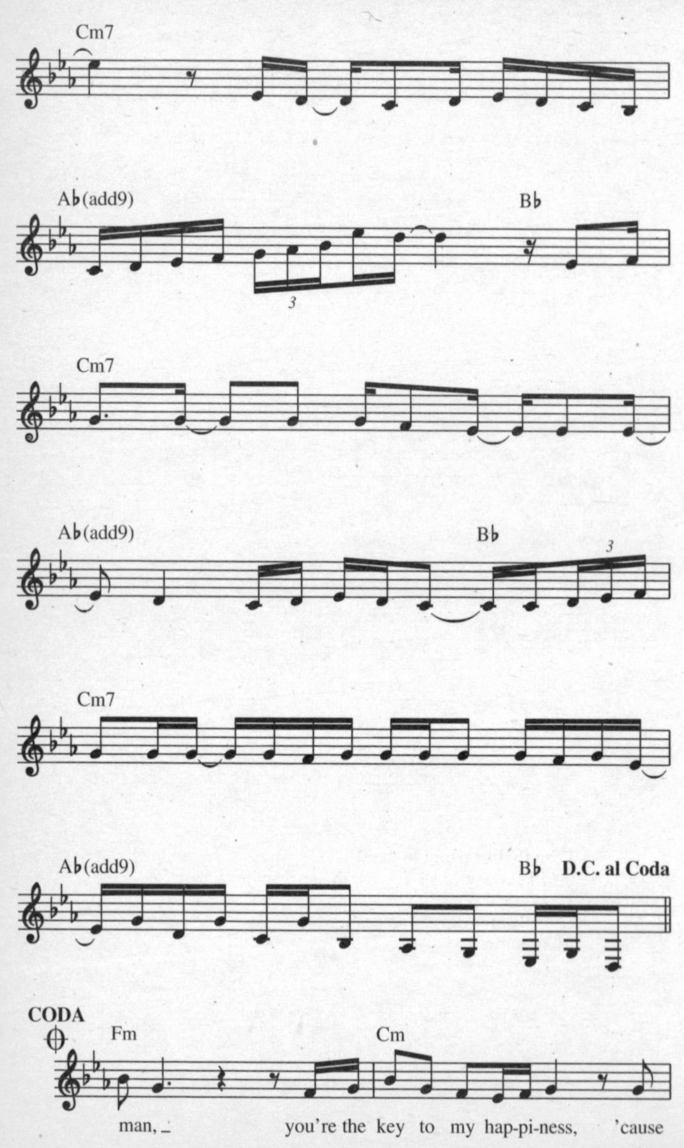
Cm7
A♭(add9)
B♭
3
Cm7
A♭(add9)
B♭
3
Cm7
A♭(add9)
B♭ D.C. al Coda
CODA
Fm
Cm
man, _ you're the key to my hap-pi-ness, 'cause

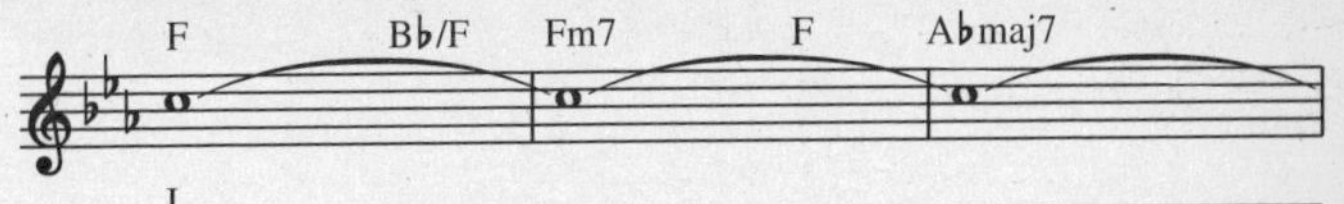
F
B♭/F
Fm7
F
A♭maj7
I

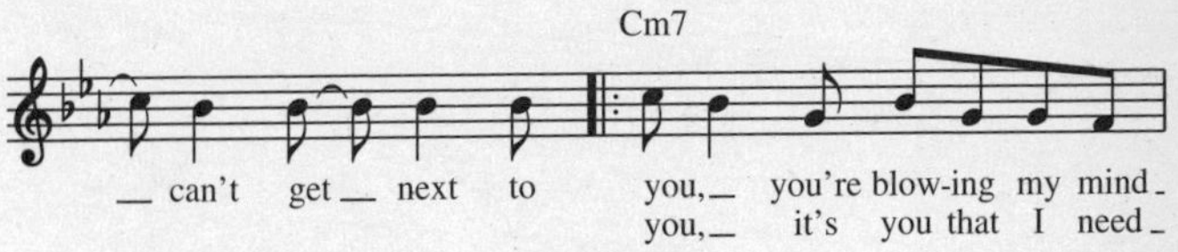
Cm7
can't get next to you, you're blow-ing my mind
you, it's you that I need

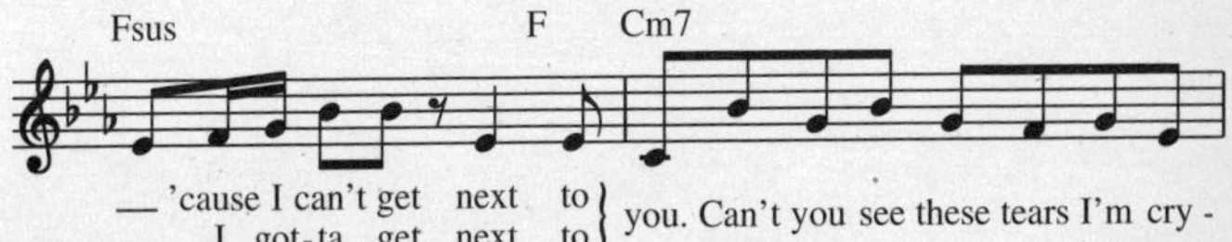
Fsus
F
Cm7
'cause I can't get next to
I got-ta get next to
you. Can't you see these tears I'm cry -

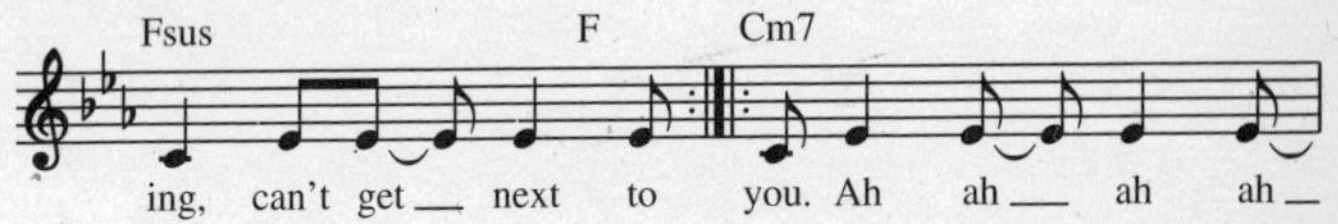
Fsus
F
Cm7
ing, can't get next to you. Ah ah ah ah

F7
Play 4 times
Cm7
ah ah.
I can't get next to you.

Additional Lyrics

2. I can fly like a bird in the sky
   And I can buy anything that money can buy.
   I can turn a river into a raging fire
   I can live forever if I so desire.
   I don't want it, all these things I can do
   'Cause I can't get next to you.

3. I can turn back the hands of time - you better believe I can
   I can make the seasons change just by waving my hand.
   I can change anything from old to new
   The thing I want to do the most I'm unable to do.
   I'm an unhappy woman with all the powers I possess
   'Cause man, you're the key to my happiness.

I CAN'T STOP LOVING YOU

Words and Music by
DON GIBSON

Slowly
C
C7
Those hap - py hours that we once
F
C
knew, though long a - go,
D7
G7
still make me blue. They say that
C
C7
time heals a bro - ken
F
C
heart, but time has stood still
G7
C
F/G
C
C7
since we've been a - part.
I can't stop
I can't stop

F
3
lov - ing you, so I've made up my
lov - ing you, there's no use to
C G7
mind to live in mem - o - ry
try. Pre-tend there's some - one new;
C C7
of old lone-some times. I can't stop
I can't live a lie. I can't stop
F 3 C
want - ing you, it's use-less to say,
want - ing you the way that I do.
G7
so I'll just live my life in
There's on - ly been one love for
1
C F/G
dreams of yes - ter - day.
me, that one love is
C G7
Those hap - py
2
C F C
you.

I GOT A WOMAN

Words and Music by
RAY CHARLES

town.
hug - gin'
town.
She's good to
just for
She's good to
Bb7
me.
her.
me.
Oh
Oh
Oh
yeah!
yeah!
yeah!
Now she's my
When I say
Some - day we'll
Eb7
dream - boat,
ba - by,
mar - ry,
oh, yes in -
please take my
don't you un - der -
deed.
hand,
stand,
She's just the
she holds me
'cause she's my
Ab7
Ab9
kind of
tight.
on - ly
girl I
She's my
lov - er
Ab7
need.
lov - er girl.
girl.

E♭
I found a wom - an

way o - ver town,

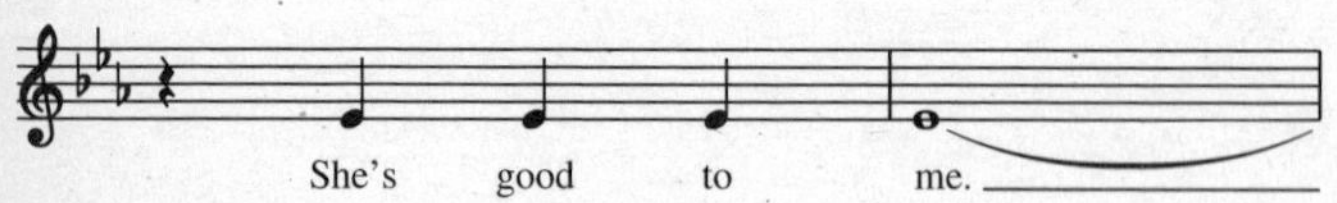
She's good to me.

A♭7
1
E♭
Oh
yeah!

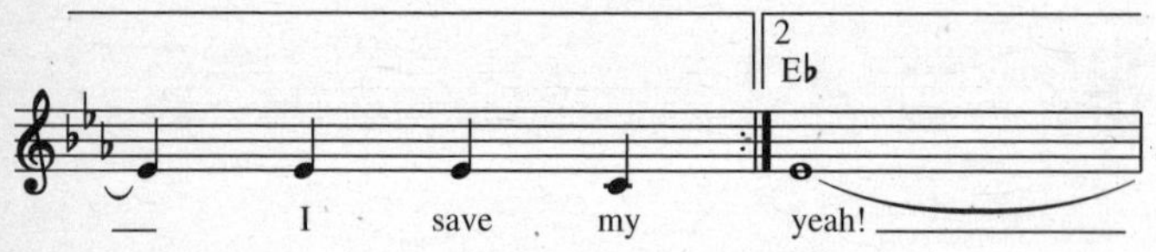
2
E♭
I save my
yeah!

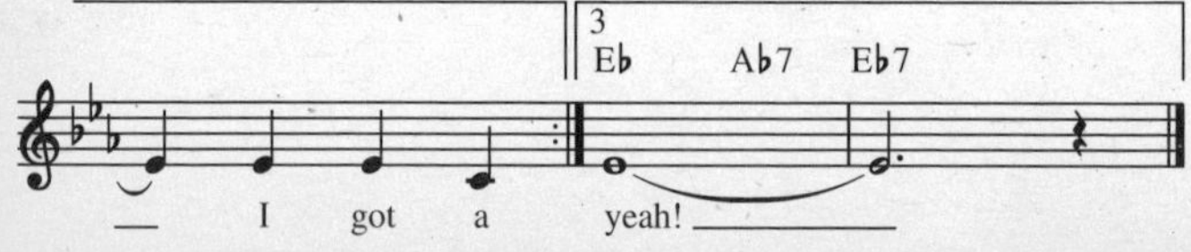
3
E♭ A♭7 E♭7
I got a
yeah!

I GOT YOU
(I Feel Good)

Words and Music by
JAMES BROWN

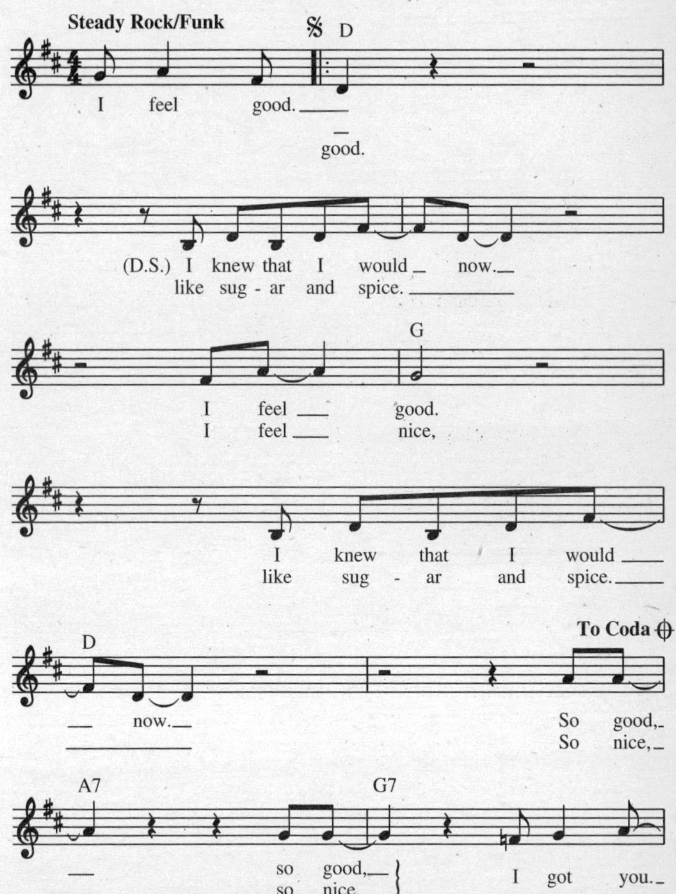

1
D N.C.
(Instrumental)
Wow!
I feel nice,
2,3
D N.C.
(Instrumental)
When I
G7
hold you in my arms I
D
know that I can't do no wrong; and

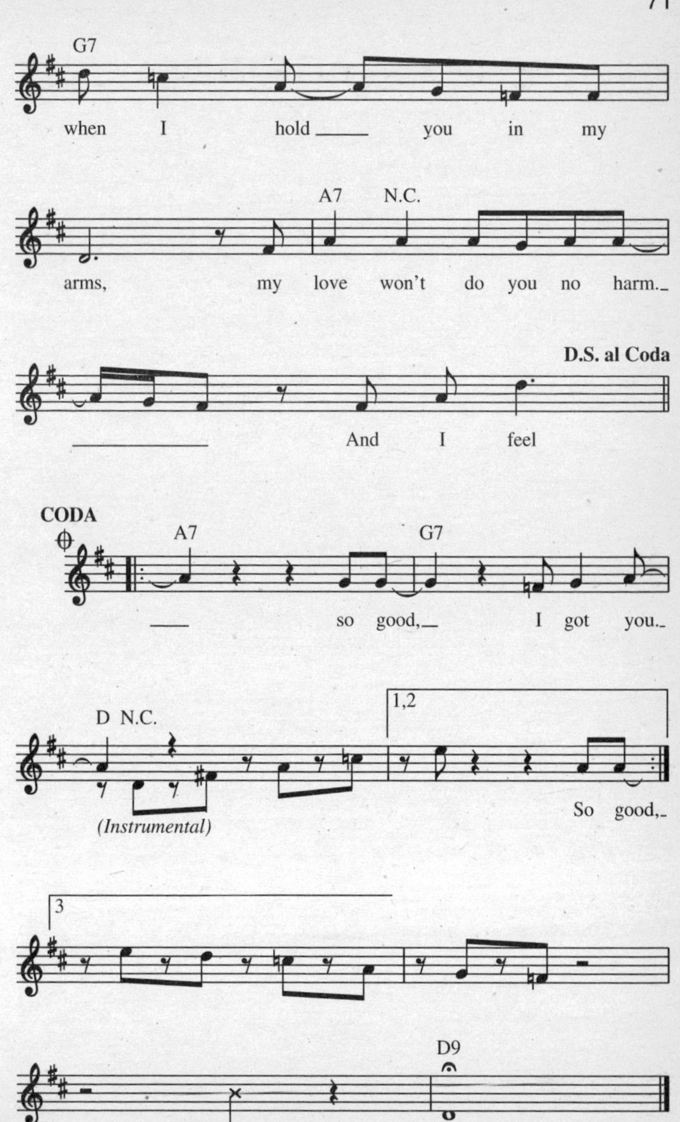
G7
when I hold ___ you in my
A7 N.C.
arms, my love won't do you no harm._
D.S. al Coda
___ And I feel
CODA
A7
G7
___ so good,_ I got you._
D N.C.
1,2
So good,_
(Instrumental)
3
D9
Hey!

I HEARD IT THROUGH THE GRAPEVINE

Words and Music by NORMAN J. WHITFIELD
and BARRETT STRONG

Moderately
Em
Em
Mm. I bet you're won-derin' how I knew
2. ain't sup-posed to cry,
3. (See additional lyrics)
B
A7
'bout your plans to make me blue,
but these tears I can't hold in - side.
Em
with some oth - er guy you knew be - fore.
Los - in' you would end my life you see,
B
Be - tween the two of us guys
'cause you mean
A7
you know I loved you more. It took me by sur -
that much to me. You could have told
C#m
A7
prise I must say when I
me your - self that you

Em
A7
found out yes - ter - day. Don't you know that I heard
loved some - one else. In - stead I heard
Em
A7
Em
A
it through the grape - vine, not much long -
it through the grape - vine, not much long -
Em
- er would you be mine. Uh huh,
- er would you be mine. Oh, I heard
A7
Em
heard it through the grape - vine. Oh, I'm just
it through the grape - vine. And I'm just
A7
a - bout to lose my mind.
a - bout to lose my mind.
Em
Hon-ey, hon-ey oh yeah.
(I heard it through the grape-vine, not much
long - er would you be mine, ba -

Additional Lyrics

3. People say believe half of what you see
Oh, and none of what you hear;
But I can't help but be confused
If it's true please tell me dear.
Do you plan to let me go
For the other guy you loved before?

I'LL COME RUNNING BACK TO YOU

Words and Music by
WILLIAM COOK

Moderately

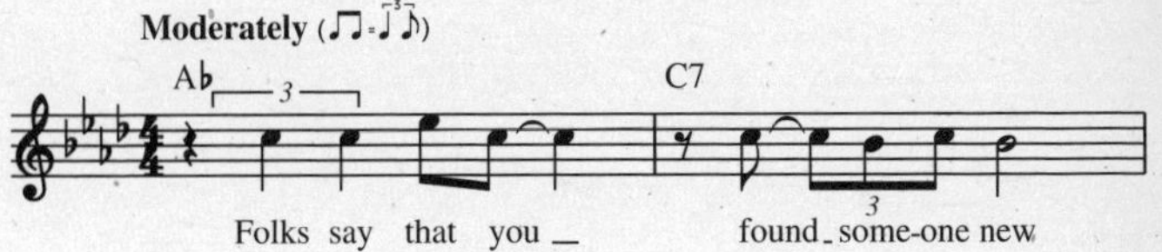
Ab
C7
Folks say that you _ found _ some-one new

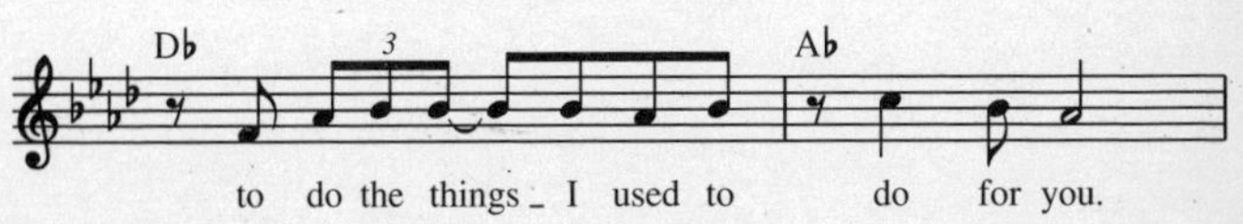
Db
Ab
to do the things _ I used to do for you.

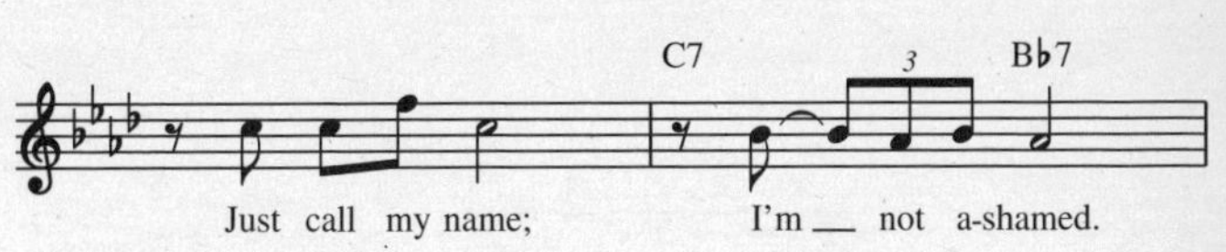
C7
Bb7
Just call my name; I'm _ not a-shamed.

Ab
Eb
I'll come run-nin' back to you. _

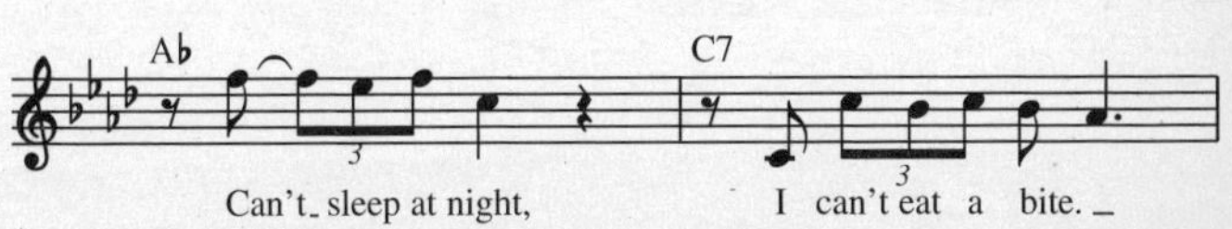
Ab
C7
Can't _ sleep at night, I can't eat a bite. _

D♭
3
A♭
When you were mine, I did-n't treat you right.

C7
B♭7
3
Just call my name, I know, I know I'm not a-shamed.

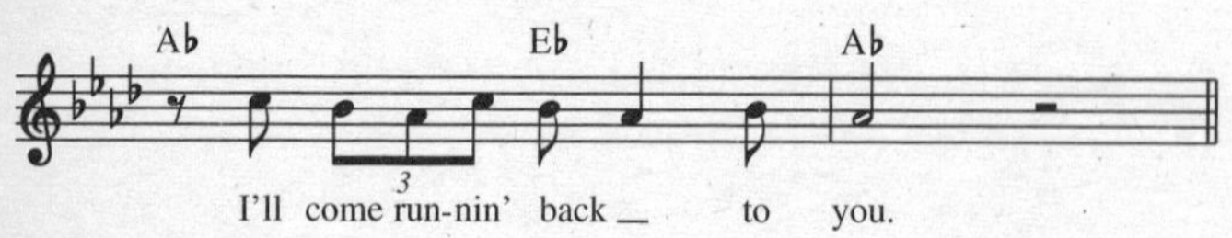
A♭
E♭
A♭
3
I'll come run-nin' back to you.

A♭9
Just like a king, I've lost ev - 'ry-thing.

D♭
C B
3
I sit all a-lone on my throne.

B♭
I've got my pride, but deep down in-side

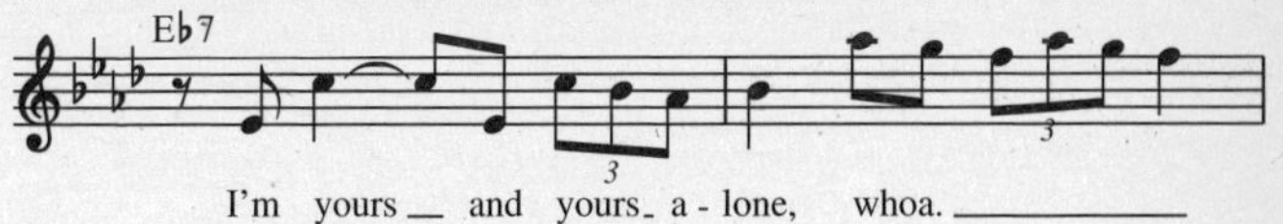
E♭7
I'm yours and yours a - lone, whoa.

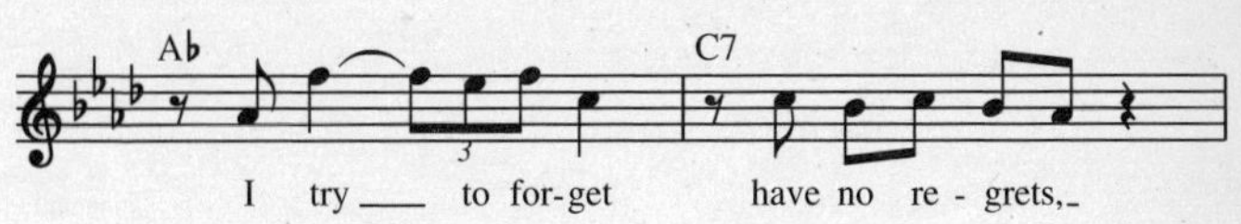
A♭
C7
I try to for-get have no re - grets,

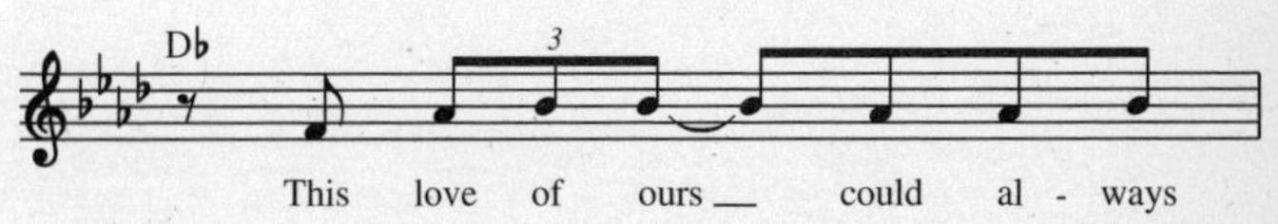
D♭
This love of ours could al - ways

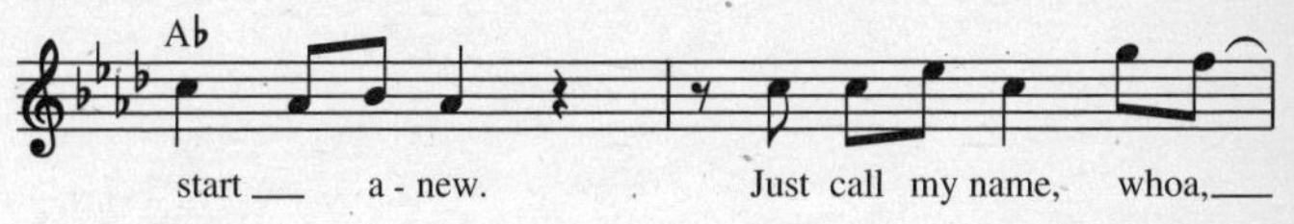
A♭
start a - new. Just call my name, whoa,

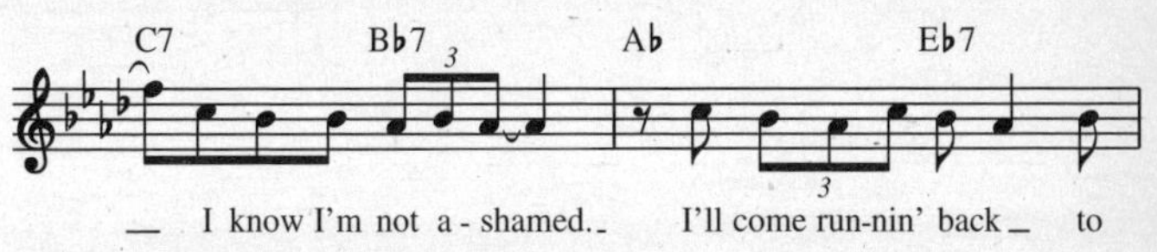
C7
B♭7
A♭
E♭7
I know I'm not a - shamed. I'll come run-nin' back to

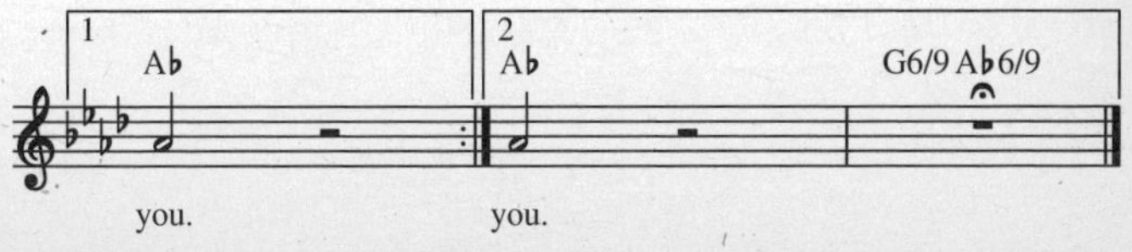
1
A♭
2
A♭
G6/9 A♭6/9
you.
you.

I THANK YOU

Words and Music by ISAAC HAYES
and DAVID PORTER

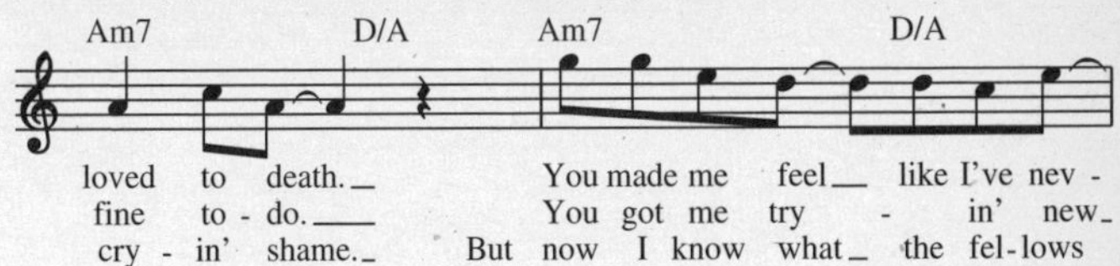
Am7
D/A
Am7
D/A
loved to death. You made me feel like I've nev -
fine to - do. You got me try - in' new
cry - in' shame. But now I know what the fel-lows

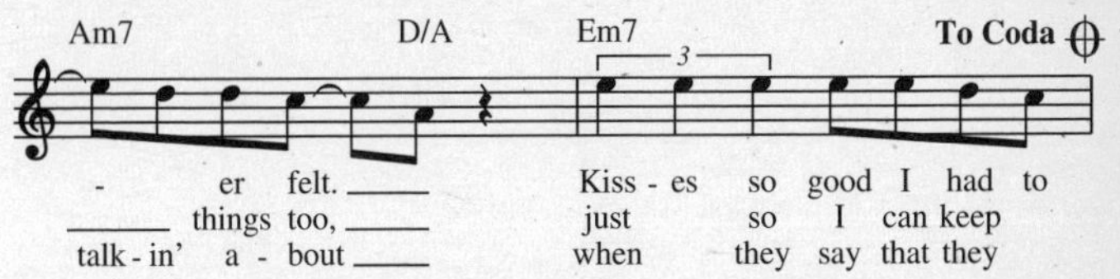
Am7
D/A
Em7
To Coda
- er felt. Kiss - es so good I had to
things too, just so I can keep
talk - in' a - bout when they say that they

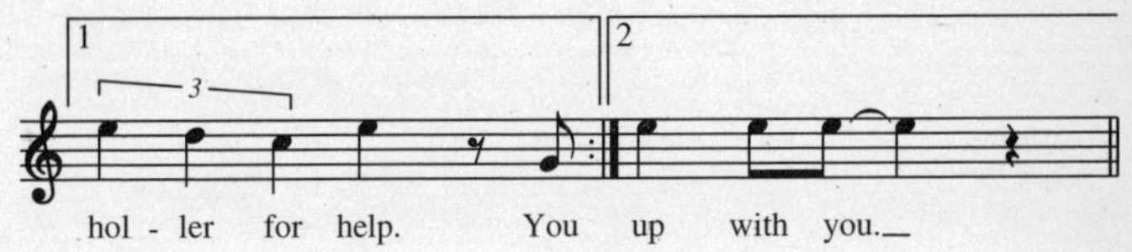
1
2
hol - ler for help. You up with you.

Am7
G
D
Play 3 times
(Instrumental)

E7
D.S. al Coda
You

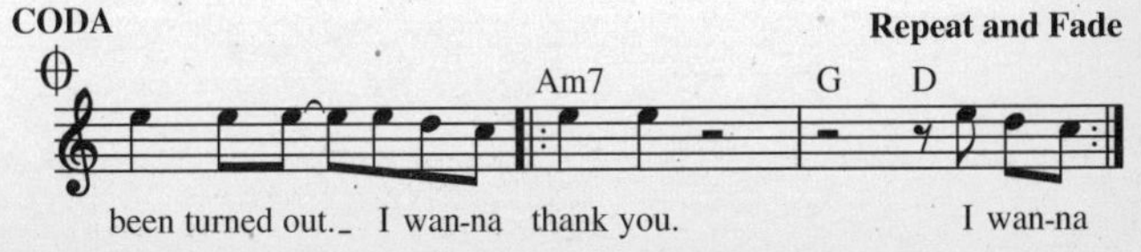
CODA
Repeat and Fade
Am7
G
D
been turned out. I wan-na thank you. I wan-na

I WISH

Words and Music by
STEVIE WONDER

Brightly

Verse

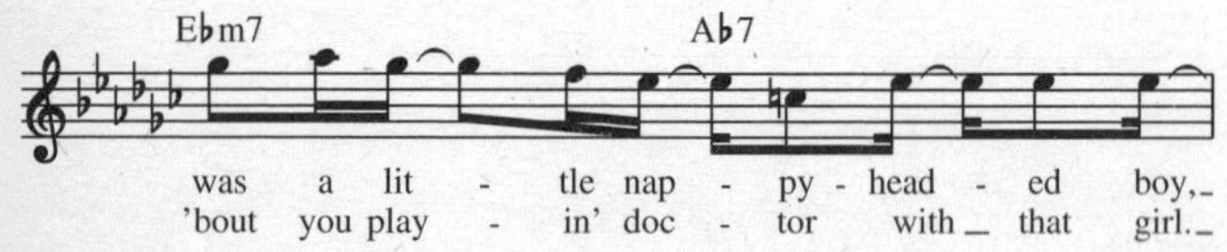

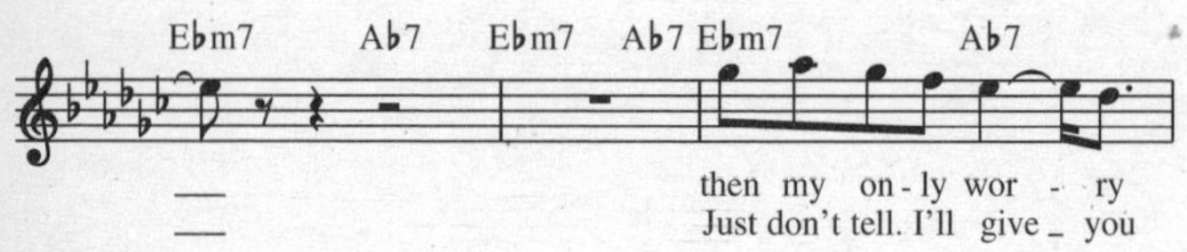

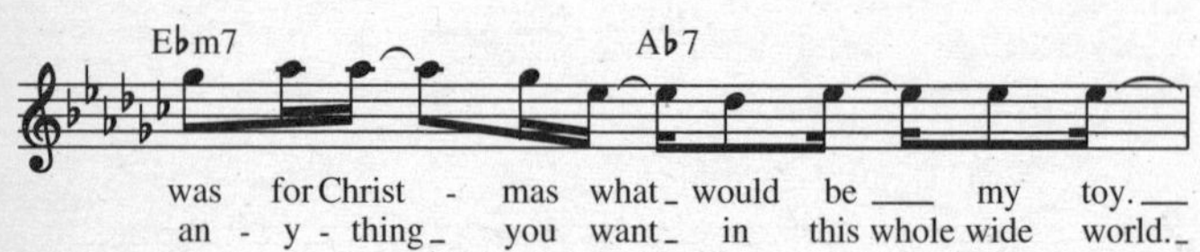

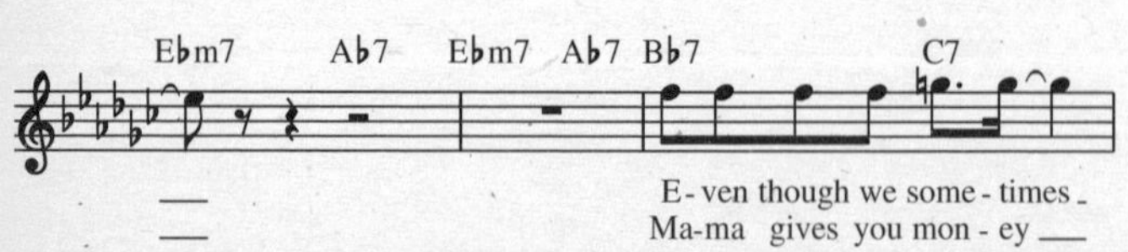

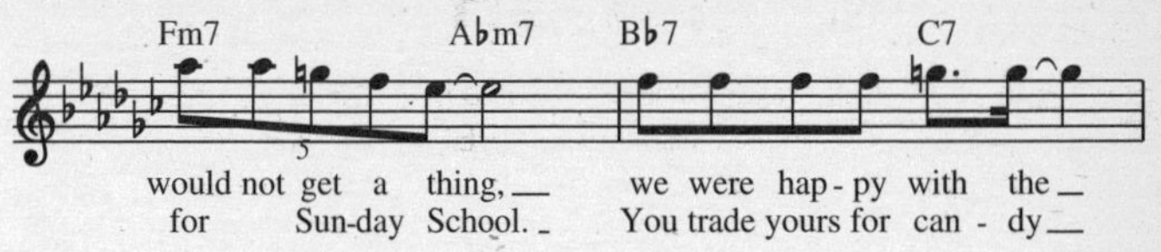
Fm7
Abm7
Bb7
C7
5
would not get a thing, we were hap-py with the
for Sun-day School. You trade yours for can - dy

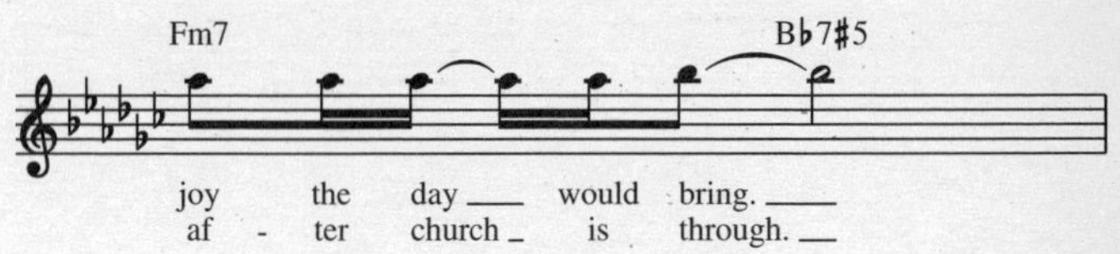
Fm7
Bb7#5
joy the day would bring.
af - ter church is through.

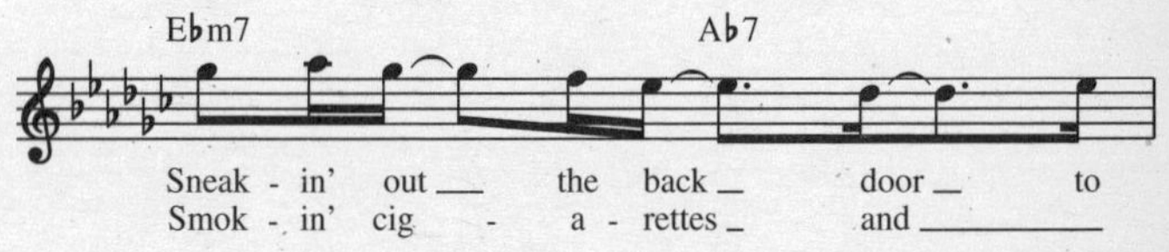
Ebm7
Ab7
Sneak - in' out the back door to
Smok - in' cig - a - rettes and

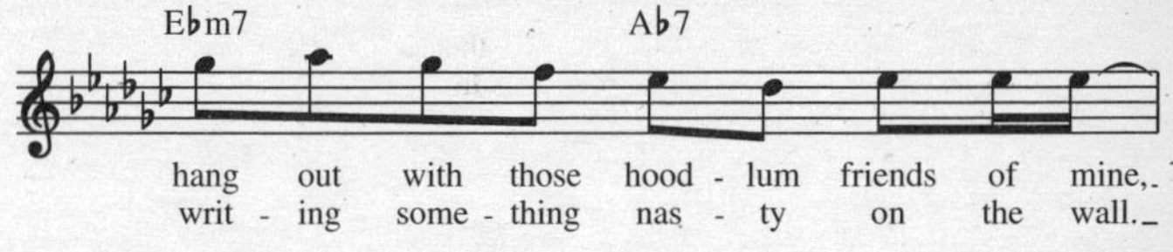
Ebm7
Ab7
hang out with those hood - lum friends of mine,
writ - ing some - thing nas - ty on the wall.

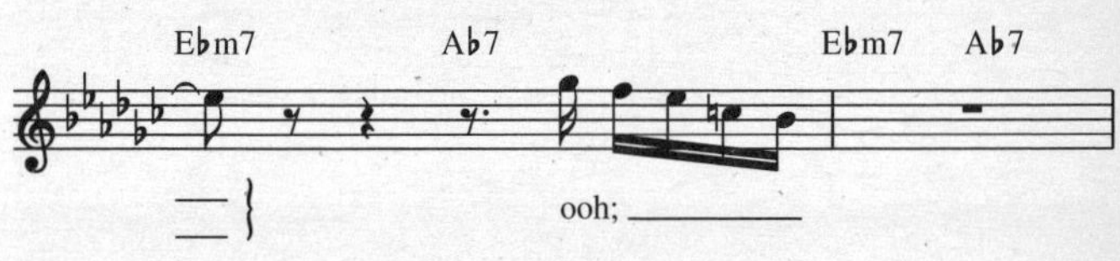
Ebm7
Ab7
Ebm7
Ab7
ooh;

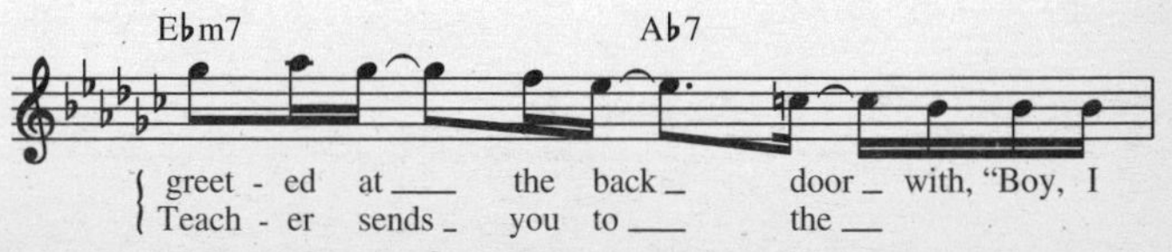
Ebm7
Ab7
greet - ed at the back door with, "Boy, I
Teach - er sends you to the

Ebm7
Ab7
thought I told you not to go out - side."
prin - ci - pal's of - fice down the hall.
Ebm7
Ab7
Ebm7
Ab7
Bb7
C7
Tryin' the best to bring the
You grow up and learn that
Fm7
Abm7
Bb7
C7
wa - ter to your eyes,
kind - a thing ain't right.
think - in' it might stop her from
But while you were do - in' it, it
Chorus
Fm7
Bb7#5
Ebm7
Ab7
whoop-in' your be - hind.
sure felt out - ta sight.
I wish those days could
Ebm7
Ab7
Ebm7
Ab7
come back once more. Why did those days ev -
Ebm7
Ab7
Ebm7
Ab7
er have to go? I wish those days could
Ebm7
Ab7
Ebm7
Ab7
come back once more. Why did those days ev -

Ebm7
Ab7
er have to go, 'cause I loved them so.
1
Ebm7
Do do do do do
do do do do do do do.
Do do do do do
do do do do do.
2
Ebm7
Ab7
Ebm7
Ab7
Repeat and Fade
Ebm7
Ab7
Ebm7
Ab7

I'LL BE YOUR SHELTER
(In Time of Storm)

Words and Music by CARL HAMPTON,
HOMER BANKS and RAYMOND JACKSON

C F/C
I will see you through. I will see you through.
C F/C
I will see you through, I will see you through.
C G C
I'll see you through your hang ups. I'll see you through your
F G C
fears. I'll see you through sad times.
F G Am G
Hon-ey, I'll dry all your tears. And when the tem-pest is-n't
F Am G
rag - ing, I want you to know you got a friend that's
F C F/C
true. Just like the shel - ter in the time of storm, I'll see you
Repeat and Fade
C F/C
through, that's what I'll do. Just like the

I'LL PLAY THE BLUES FOR YOU

Words and Music by
JERRY BEACH

D7
Cm
I'll try to soothe.

To Coda
I'll play the blues for

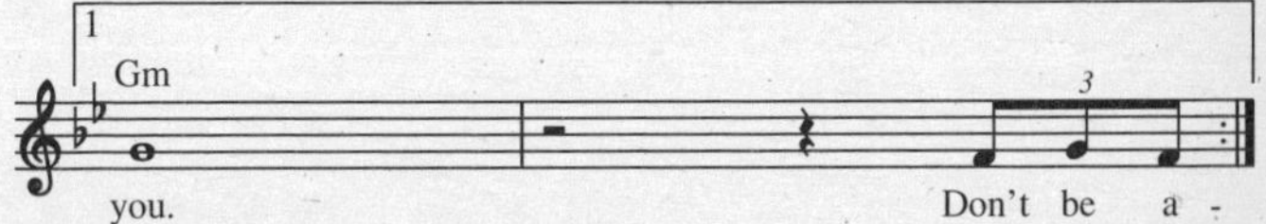
1
Gm
you.
Don't be a -

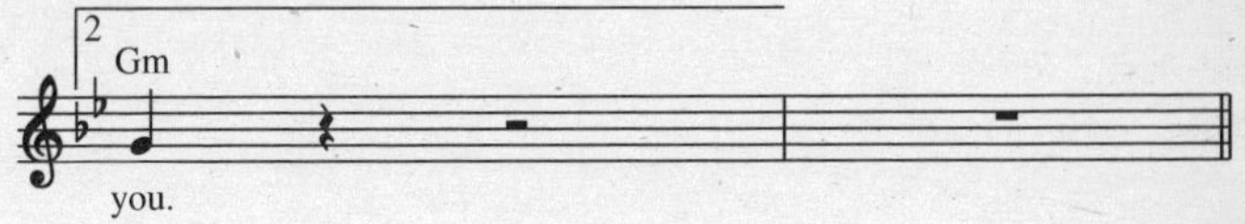
2
Gm
you.

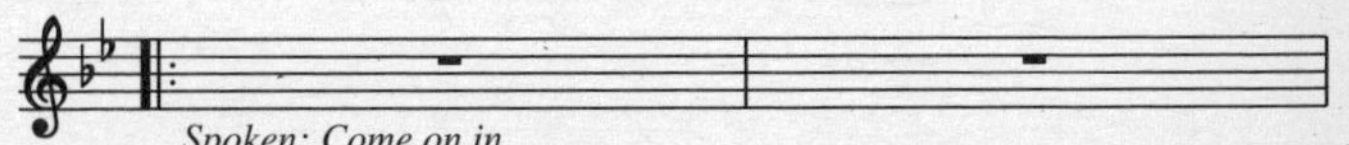
Spoken: Come on in,
good people's minds,
you know. But you can't do that.

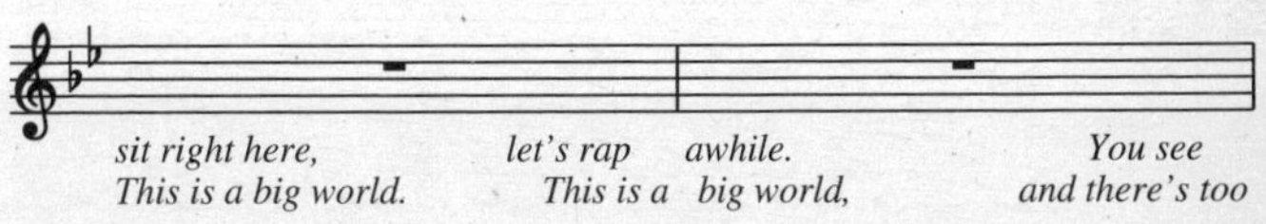
sit right here,
let's rap
awhile.
You see
This is a big world.
This is a
big world,
and there's too

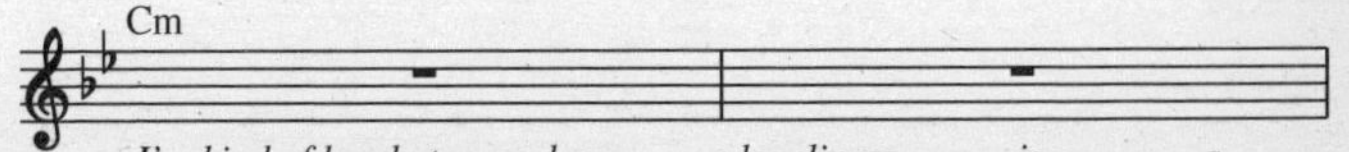
Cm
I'm kind of lonely too, and
loneliness
is
a
many nice things happening in this
world.
You're a very pretty

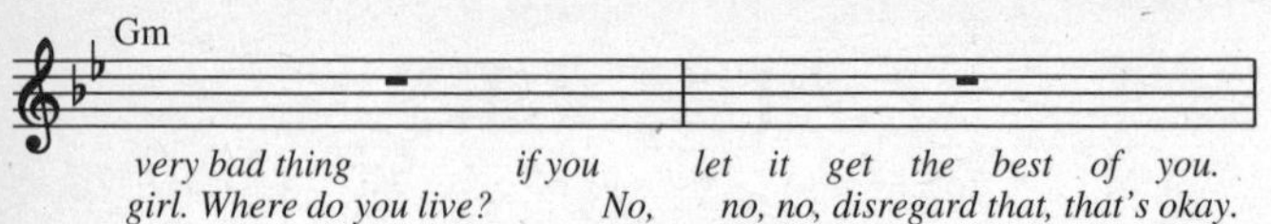
Gm
very bad thing if you let it get the best of you.
girl. Where do you live? No, no, no, disregard that, that's okay.

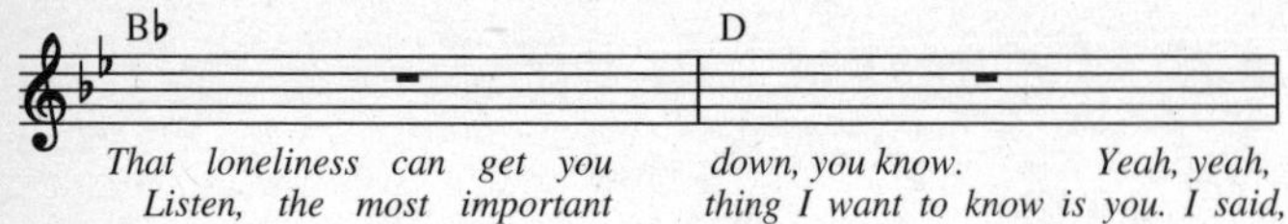
B♭
D
That loneliness can get you down, you know. Yeah, yeah,
Listen, the most important thing I want to know is you. I said,

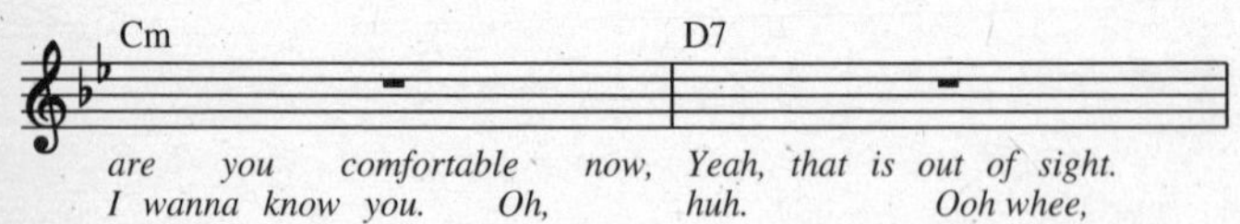
Cm
D7
are you comfortable now, Yeah, that is out of sight.
I wanna know you. Oh, huh. Ooh whee,

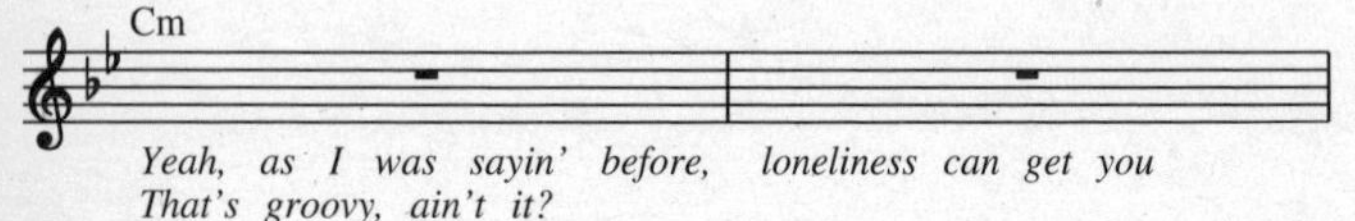
Cm
Yeah, as I was sayin' before, loneliness can get you
That's groovy, ain't it?

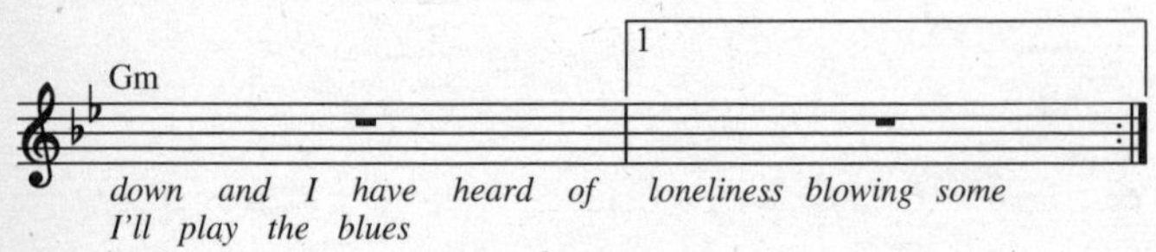
1
Gm
down and I have heard of loneliness blowing some
I'll play the blues

2
D.S. al Coda
CODA
for you. I ain't
you.

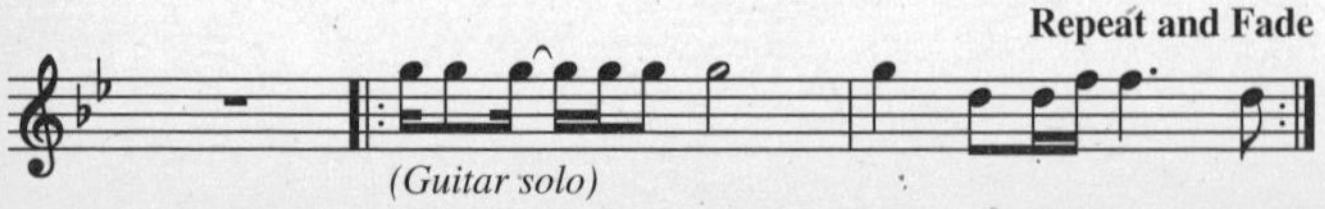
Repeat and Fade
(Guitar solo)

I'M STILL IN LOVE WITH YOU

Words and Music by AL GREEN,
WILLIE MITCHELL and AL JACKSON, JR.

Moderately
C
Spend - ing my days
Cm7
Am7
3
think-ing a - bout you girl.
Gmaj7
Be - ing
G7
here with you, be-ing here with you I can't ex -
C
plain my - self, why
Cm7
Am7
I feel like I
Gmaj7
do. 'Tho it

G7
hurt me so to let you know. And I
C
look in your eyes and you
Cm7 Am7 Gmaj7
let me know how you feel.
all the years. How I see
G7
Let me know that
me lov-ing you and
Cm7
love is real-ly real and it seems to me
you lov-ing me, it seems to me
Am7
that I'm
Cm7
wrapped up in your love.
Cmaj7 C Bm
Don't you know that I'm still in love, sho -

To Coda
Am7
D7
E♭
nuff in love with you.
Instrumental solo
F
G
C
Bm
Well I know that I'm still in love sho -
Am7
D7
Dm7
Em
nuff in love with you.
D.S. al Coda
CODA
Dm7
G7
Cm7
When I
I
Am7
I
Cm7
Cmaj7
don't you now that I'm
Repeat and Fade
C
Bm
Am7
D7
still in love sho - nuff in love with you.

I'LL TAKE YOU THERE

Words and Music by
ALVERTIS ISBELL

C F F/G
rac - es). Ain't no - bod - y cry - ing, no more
C F F/G
cry - ing. If you're read - y now
C F F/G
Female:
come on, come on, (I'll take you there.) Lord have mer -
C
Male:
Say if you read - y (I'll take you
cy.
F F/G C
there.) Oh, yeah. (I'll take you
Help me, help me,
F F/G
there.) Come on I said
Help me.
C
come on (I'll take you)
F7 C
there.
Vocal and instrumental solos ad lib.

Play 4 times
F F/G C F F/G
C F
(Vocal/instrumental)
C
1
F
Female:
If you're read - y now.
2
F C N.C.
Female:
Oh I, oh,
F C N.C.
I, I know a place ya'll,
F C N.C. C
oh, there ain't no - bod - y cry-ing.
F Male: F/G C
Say ain't no (Ain't no - bod - y cry - ing.) I said,
F F/G
I said ain't no,
(ain't no - bod - y

C F F/G
wor - ried, yeah.) (Ain't no smil - ing
C F F/G
No smil - ing fac - es ly - ing to the rac - es,
fac - es.)
C
help me now. (I'll take you
F F/G C
there.) I said if you're read - y (I'll take you
F F/G C
there.) I said (I'll take you
F F/G C
there.) Come on get read - y. (I'll take you
F F/G C
there. Come, go with me.) (Vocal ad lib.)
F F/G C
Repeat and Fade ad lib.
(Come, go with

I'M LOSING YOU
(I Know)

Words and Music by CORNELIUS GRANT,
NORMAN WHITFIELD and EDWARD HOLLAND

Moderately bright
D
Your love ___ is fad - in', I can
F/D
G/D
feel your love fad - in'. Wom-an, it's fad - in' a -
F/D
D
way from me. 'Cause your bash - ful touch _ has grown
F/D
cold, as if ___ some-one else con-trolled your ver -
D
C/D
G/D
D
- y soul. _ I fooled my - self ___
long as I can. ________ I can
feel the pres - ence ___ of an - oth -

F
- er man.
It' s
D
F/D
there when you speak my name,
it's just not the same
G/D
F/D
oh ___ hon - ey, I'm los - ing you.
I can
D
F/D
feel it in _ the air,
it's there ev-'ry-where, ___
G/D
Oh, ___ hon - ey I'm
F/D
los - ing you.
I can
D
feel it in ___ my bones, _
an - y
look in - to ___ your eyes, _
a re -

F/D
G/D
day you'll be up and gone. Ooh, I'm
flec - tion of a face I see. Oh, Lord, I'm
F/D
1
D
los - ing you. It's all o - ver your face, some-one's
los - ing you. I'm
F/D
tak - in' my place. Could it
G/D
F/D
be that I'm los - ing you? When I
2
D
hurt, down-heart-ed and wor-ried, girl, 'cause that
face does - n't be - long to me.
Ooh Hm hm
N.C.
hm hm

D
hm.
your love is fad - in',
F
I can feel it fad - in',
G/D
F/D
Oh a - way from me. I can
D
feel it in the air, it's
I don't wan - na lose you, but I
F/D
G/D
there ev - 'ry-where, ooh, I'm
know I'm gon - na groove you. Oh, Lord I'm
F/D
D
los - ing you.
los - ing you.
Your love is fad - in',
F/D
I can feel it fad - in'
G/D
D
F
Oh Lord, I'm los - ing you.

I'VE BEEN LOVING YOU TOO LONG

Words and Music by OTIS REDDING
and JERRY BUTLER

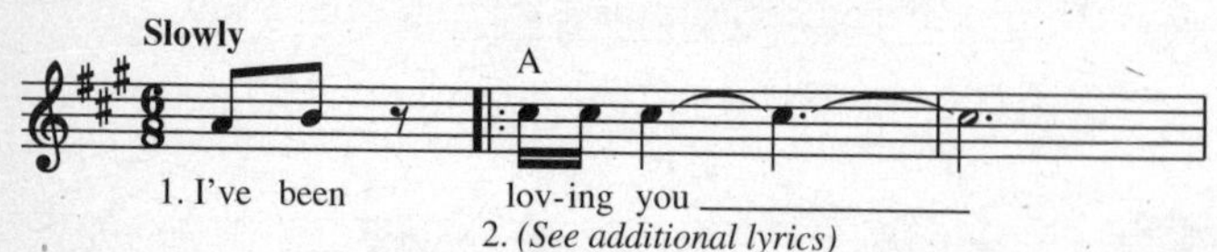
Slowly
A
1. I've been lov-ing you
2. (See additional lyrics)

E
too long

A
to stop now.

E
A
You are tired

C#
and you want to be free.

D
My love is grow-ing strong - er,

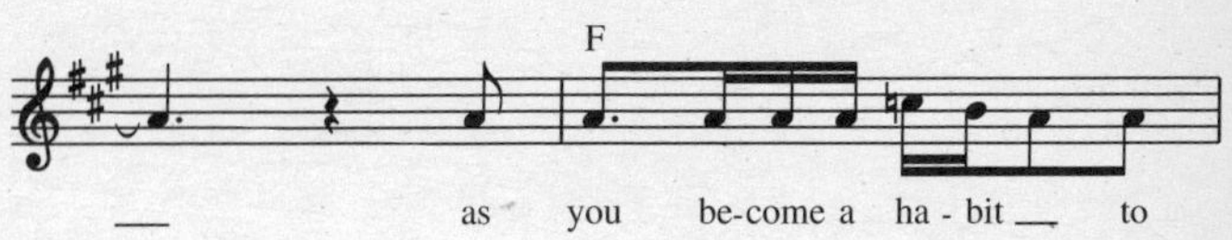
F
as you be-come a ha - bit to

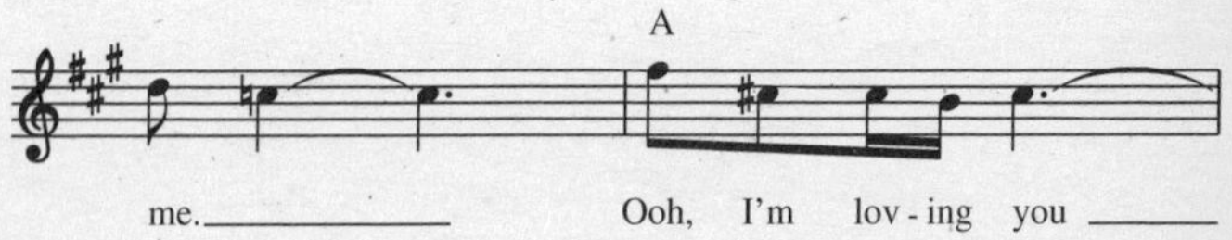
A
me.
Ooh, I'm lov - ing you

E
a lit - tle too long.

A
I don't wan - na stop now.

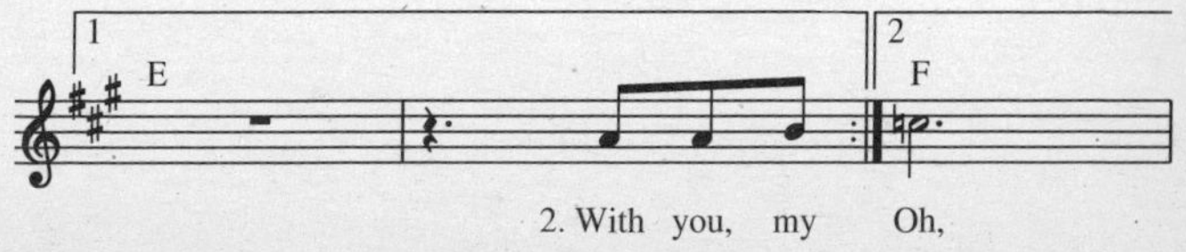
1
E
2
F
2. With you, my
Oh,

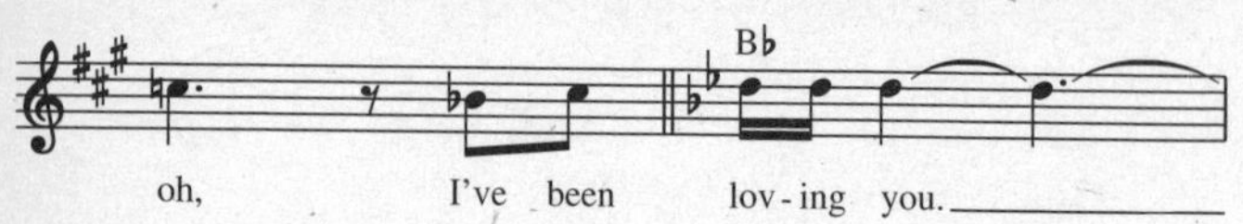
B♭
oh, I've been lov - ing you.

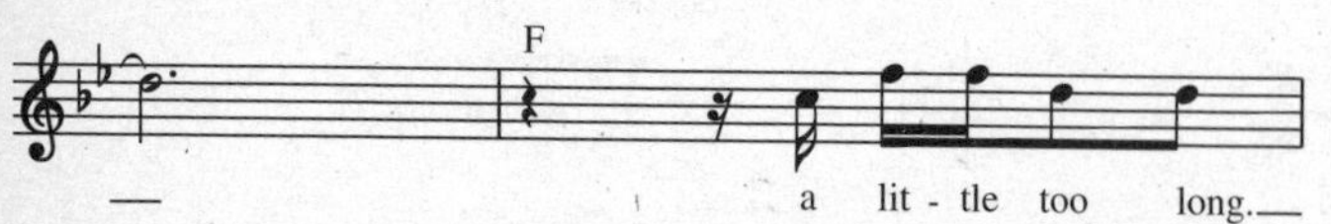
F
a lit - tle too long.

B♭
I don't wan-na stop now.

G♭
Oh, oh, and don't make me

Repeat and Fade
(Vocal ad lib.)
B♭
stop now.

Additional Lyrics

2. With you, my life has been so wonderful;
I can't stop now.
You are tired,
And your love is growing cold;
My love is growing stronger,
As our affair grows old.
I've been loving you, a little too long;
I don't wanna stop now.

LET'S GET IT ON

Words and Music by MARVIN GAYE
and ED TOWNSEND

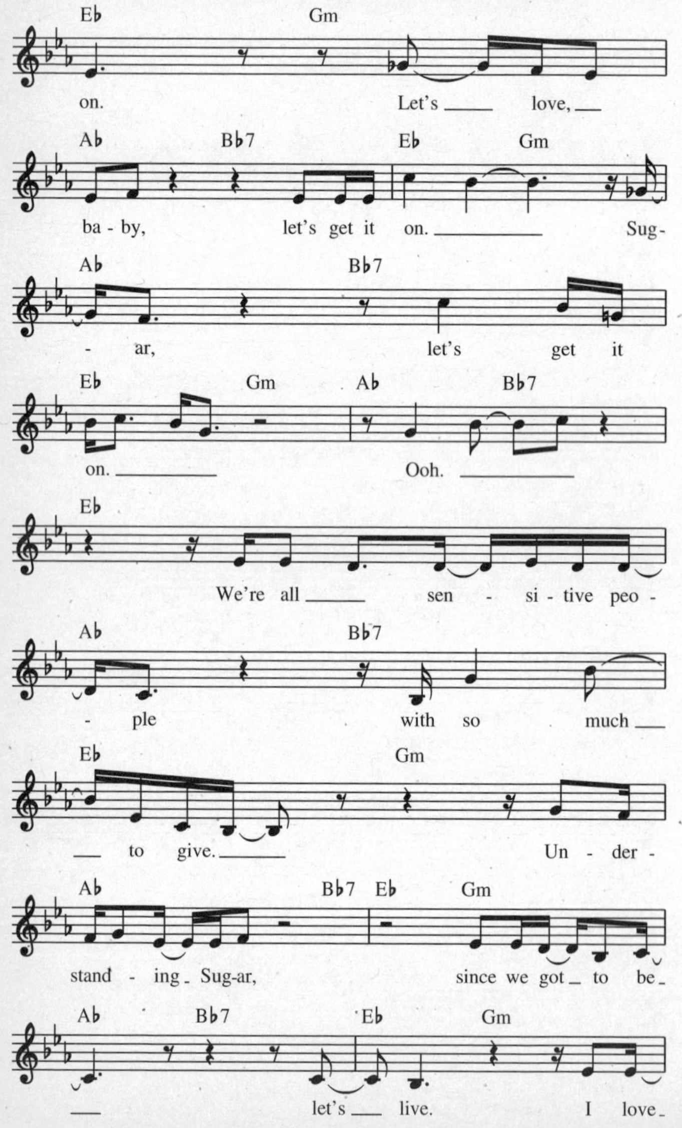
E♭
Gm
on.
Let's love,
A♭
B♭7
E♭
Gm
ba - by,
let's get it
on.
Sug-
A♭
B♭7
- ar,
let's
get
it
E♭
Gm
A♭
B♭7
on.
Ooh.
E♭
We're all
sen
-
si - tive peo -
A♭
B♭7
- ple
with
so
much
E♭
Gm
to
give.
Un
-
der -
A♭
B♭7
E♭
Gm
stand - ing Sug-ar,
since we got to
be
A♭
B♭7
E♭
Gm
let's
live.
I
love

Ab Bb7 Eb Gm
you. There's noth - in' wrong
Ab Bb7
with me lov - in'
Eb Gm
you, Ba - by, no, no.
Ab Bb7
And
Eb Gm
giv - in' your - self to me can nev - er be wrong
Ab Bb7
if the love is
Eb Gm Ab Bb7
true. Oh, ba - by, ooh.
Ab
Don't you know how sweet and won-der-ful
Eb Gm
life can be. Ooh,

A♭
E♭7
A♭
ooh.
I'm
ask - in' you,
ba - by,
to get it on with me.
E♭
Gm
Ooh,
ooh,
A♭
B♭7
ooh.
A♭
I ain't goin' to wor -
- ry.
I ain't goin' to push.
E♭
Gm
A♭
B♭
I won't push you, ba - by.
Just
A♭
come on, come on, come on, come on, come on, come on ba -
Fm
- by,
stop beat - in' 'round the

Bb7
— bush.
Hey, —
let's get
Eb
Gm
it on.
Ooh, —
ooh. —
Ab
Bb7
let's get it
Eb
Gm
on. —
You — know —
what I'm
Ab
Bb7
talk - in' a - bout. —
Come on, — ba -
Eb
Gm
- by.
Hey, —
hey, —
Ab
Bb7
Eb
Gm
let your love come — out.
If you
Ab
Bb7
be - lieve — in love, — let's get it on. —
Eb
Gm
Ab
Bb7
Ooh. —
let's get it on, — ba -

E♭
Gm
- by, this min - ute.
A♭
B♭7
Oh, yeah, let's get it on.
E♭
Gm
A♭
B♭7
Ee, please
E♭
Gm
A♭
B♭7
get it on. Hey, hey.
A♭
Come on, come on, come on, come on, come on, dar -
Fm
- lin', stop beat - in' 'round the bush.
B♭7
Oh, gon - na get it on.
E♭
Gm
Right with you,

Ab
Bb7
ba - by, I want to get it on.
Eb
Gm
Ab
Bb7
You don't have to wor - ry that it's wrong.
Eb
Gm
If the spi - rit moves you, let me groove
Ab
Bb7
you. Good, let your love come
Eb
Gm
Ab
Bb7
down, oh. Get it on, come on,
Eb
Gm
ba - by. Do you know I
Ab
Bb7
Eb
Gm
mean it? I've been sanc - ti - fied. Hey,
Ab
Bb
Eb
Gm
hey. Girl, you give me good feel - ings, so good,
Ab
Bb7
Eb
some-thin' like sum-mer - time.

IF LOVING YOU IS WRONG I DON'T WANT TO BE RIGHT

Words and Music by HOMER BANKS,
CARL HAMPTON and RAYMOND JACKSON

Cmaj7
long as I got you by my side I don't
know - ing I got some-one - else at home who
Am7 Bm7 Cmaj7 Bm7
care what your peo - ple say. Your
needs me just as much? And
Am
friends tell you it's no fu - ture in
are you wrong to give your love
Em Am
lov-ing a mar-ried man. If I can't see you when I want, I'll
to a mar-ried man? And am I wrong for try'n' to hold on to
Em
see you when I can.
the best thing I ev - er had?
If
C
lov - ing you is wrong, I don't
Em
wan - na be right. If

C
lov - ing you is wrong, I don't

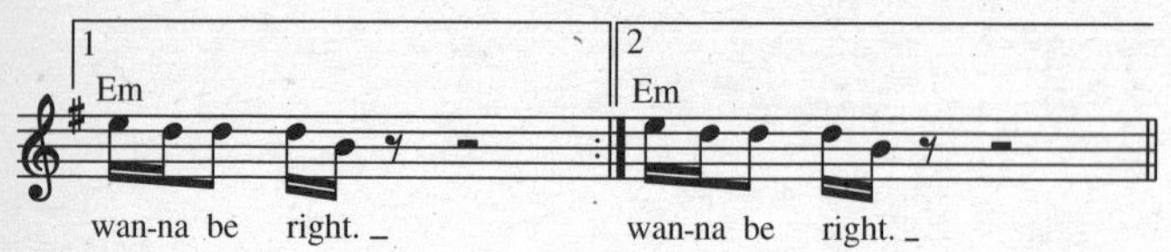
1
Em
wan-na be right.
2
Em
wan-na be right.

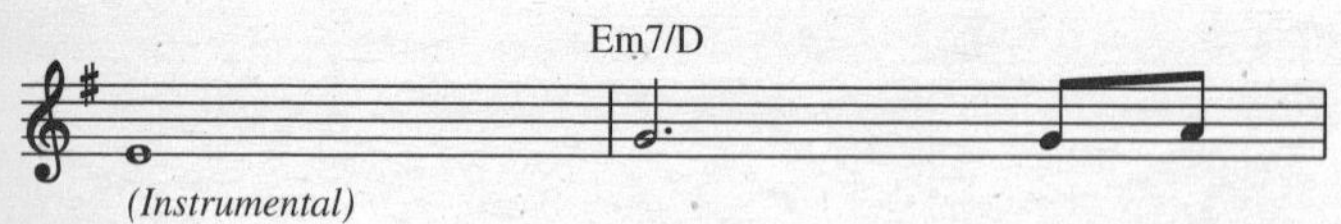
Em7/D
(Instrumental)

Cmaj7
Am7
Bm7
Cmaj7
Bm7

Am
Are you wrong to give your love

Em
to a mar - ried man? And

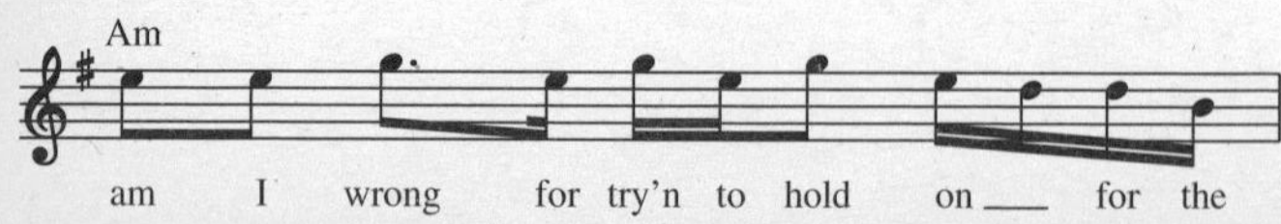
Am
am I wrong for try'n to hold on for the

Em

best thing I ev - er had? __ If

C

lov - ing you is wrong, ______ I don't

Em

wan - na be __ right. If

C

lov - ing you is wrong, ______ I don't

Em Em

wan-na be right. I don't wan - na be_ right, if it

C Em

means be-ing with-out_you. I don't wan - na be_ right if it

Repeat and Fade
(Vocal ad lib.)
C
means ______ sleep - ing at night.

IF YOU'RE READY
(Come Go with Me)

Words and Music by HOMER BANKS,
CARL HAMPTON and RAYMOND JACKSON

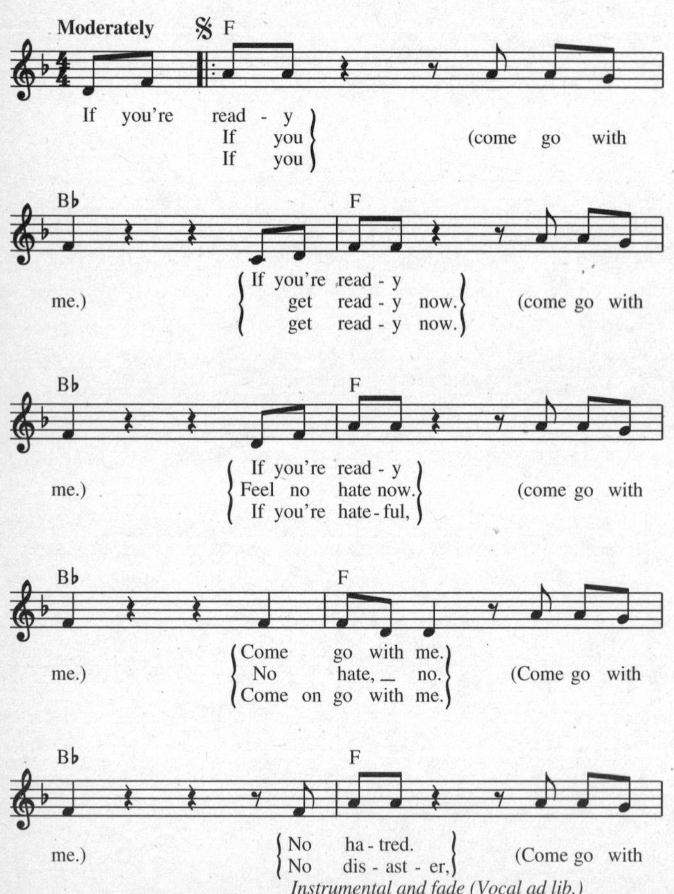

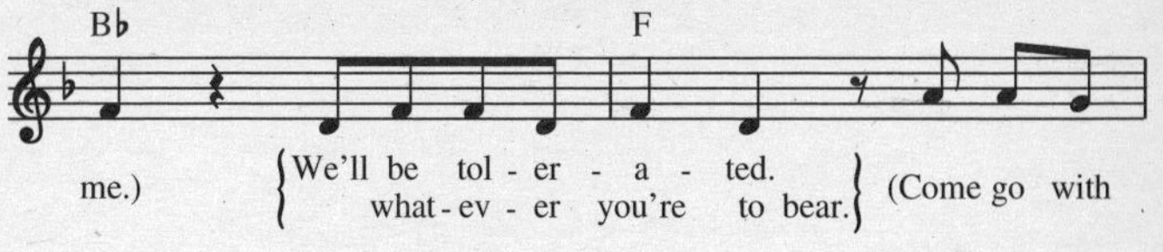
B♭
F
me.)
We'll be tol - er - a - ted.
what - ev - er you're to bear.
(Come go with

B♭
F
me.)
Peace and love
No wars
(Come go with

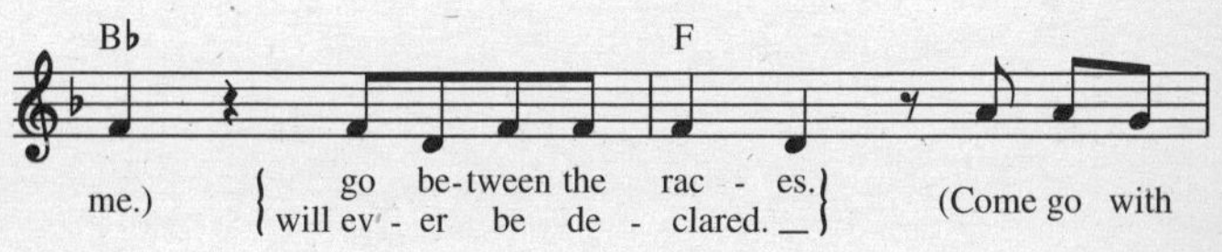
B♭
F
me.)
go be-tween the rac - es.
will ev - er be de - clared.
(Come go with

B♭
C7
me.)
Love is the on - ly
No ec - o - nom - i - cal

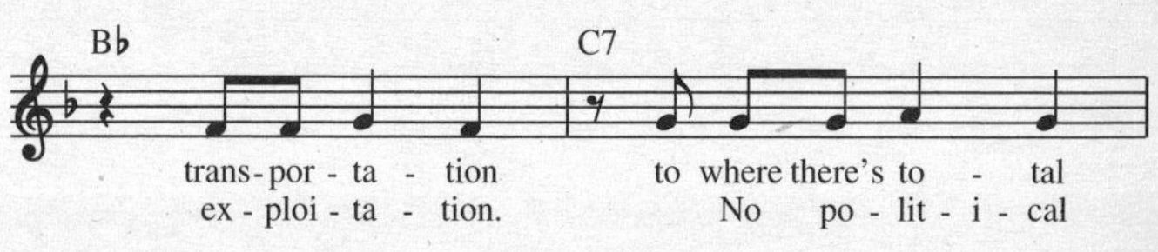
B♭
C7
trans-por - ta - tion to where there's to - tal
ex - ploi - ta - tion. No po - lit - i - cal

D.S. and Fade

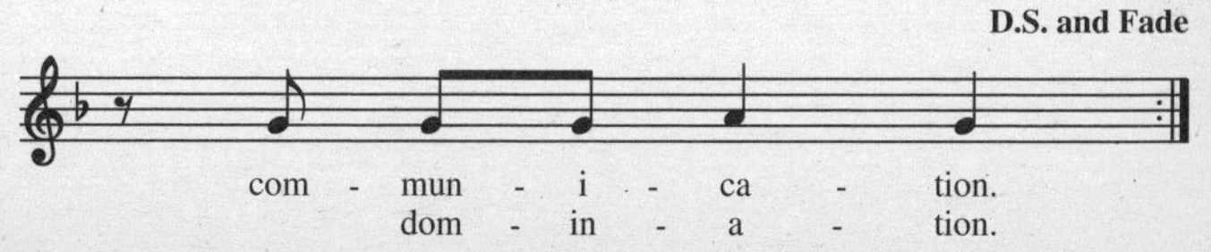
com - mun - i - ca - tion.
dom - in - a - tion.

IN THE MIDNIGHT HOUR

Words and Music by STEVE CROPPER
and WILSON PICKETT

Moderately
Bb
Eb
(1.) I'm gon - na (D.S.) wait till the mid - night hour.
(2.) wait till the stars come out,
(3.) Instrumental solo
That's when my love comes tum-bling on down.
and see the twin - kle in your eyes.
I'm gon - na wait till the mid-night hour,
I'm gon - na wait till the mid-night hour,
when there's no one else a - round.
that's where my love will be - gin to shine.
Dm7
I'm gon - na take you girl and
You are the on - ly one I
To Coda
F
Cm7
3
hold you, and do all the things I told
know that real - ly, real - ly loves me

1,2
Bb
Eb
you in the mid-night hour. Oh yeah,
so in the mid-night hour. Oh yeah,
Bb
Eb
Ab
in the mid - night hour.
in the mid - night hour.
F7
Gon - na
3
Bb
Eb
Bb
Eb
D.S. al Coda
CODA
Solo ends
I'm gon - na
you
Bb
Eb
in the mid - night hour. Oh yeah,
Bb
Eb
Bb
Eb
in the mid-night hour. Oh babe,
Repeat and Fade
(Vocal ad lib.)
Bb
Eb
Bb
Eb
Bb
Eb
you make me feel so good.

IT'S GONNA WORK OUT FINE

Words and Music by
IKE TURNER

Moderately
C
F
Dar - ling, it's time to get next to me.
I - kie, I been to see the preach-er man.
mem - ber I used to call you Dap - per Dan.
C Eb C F C Eb C F G C
Dar - ling, I
I start - ed,
The thrill - er, the
F G F#
nev - er thought that this could be, oh, yeah.
start-ed mak - in' wed-ding plans, oh, yeah.
ev - er read - y, lov - ing man, oh, yeah. A
F Eb C
Yours lips set my soul on fire. You could be my
If your love is half as true as the love I
whole lot of girls used to feel your speed, but now pret - ty dad-dy, I'm
F Bb/F F
one de - sire.
have for you, Oh, dar - lin', (yes, yes,) I
all you ned.
G C F
To Coda
think
think it's gon - na work out fine. (It's gon - na work out fine.)
know

1
C
2
C
I keep a - tell - in' ya I
F
think it's gon - na work out fine.
I
C
feel it's gon - na work out.
I
F
G
know it's gon-na work out fine.
I'm so glad that you're
D.C. al Coda
CODA
C
mine, all mine. Re-
I keep a - tell - in' ya I
F
think it's gon - na work out fine.
I
C
feel it's gon - na work out.
I
F
know it's gon - na work out fine.
I
Repeat and Fade
C
know it's gon - na work out fine.
I

KISS AND SAY GOODBYE

Words and Music by
WINDFRED LOVETT

Moderately slow

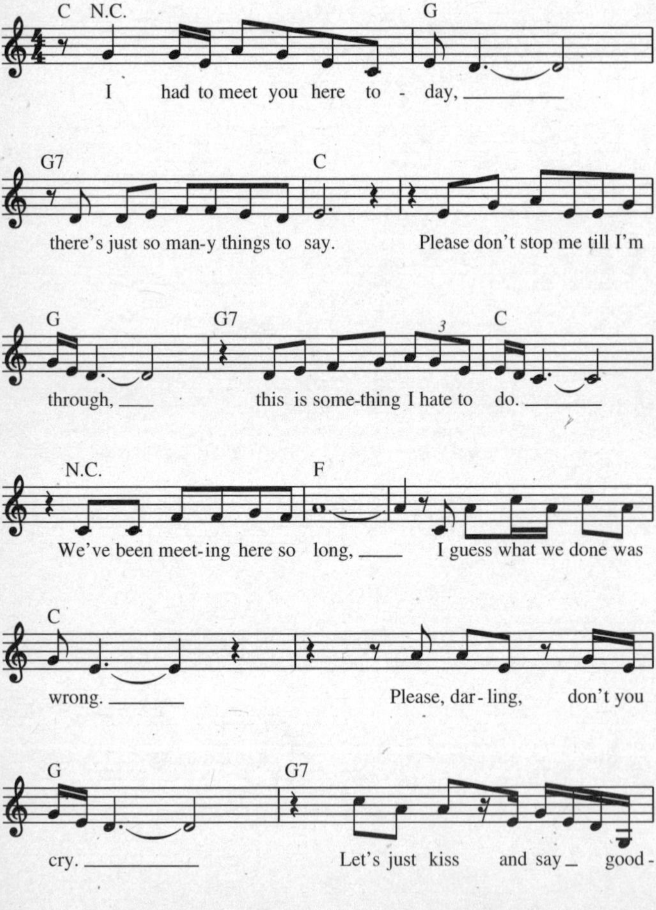

C N.C.
G
I had to meet you here to - day,
G7
C
there's just so man-y things to say. Please don't stop me till I'm
G
G7
3
C
through, this is some-thing I hate to do.
N.C.
F
We've been meet-ing here so long, I guess what we done was
C
wrong. Please, dar-ling, don't you
G
G7
cry. Let's just kiss and say good -

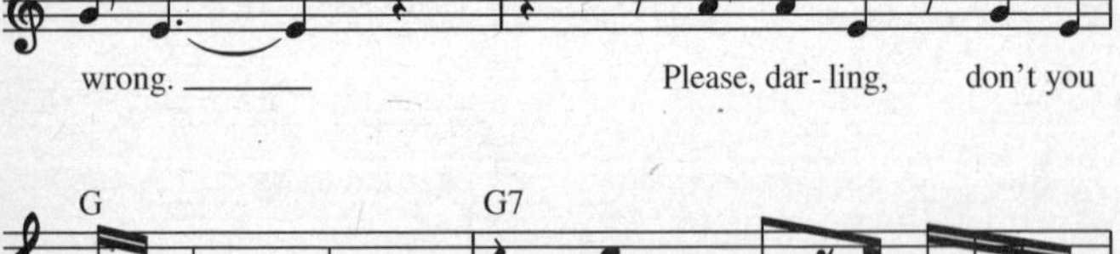

C
N.C.
bye.
Man-y months have passed us
G
G7
by,
I'm gon-na miss you
I can't
C
G
lie.
I've got ties and so do
you,
G7
C
N.C.
I just think this is the thing to do.
It's gon-na hurt me I can't
F
C
lie,
may-be you'll meet
an-oth-er
guy.
G
Un-der-stand-me
won't you
try,
try,
try.
G7
C F C Dm7 C
Let's just kiss
and say
good-bye.

KNOCK ON WOOD

Words and Music by EDDIE FLOYD
and STEVE CROPPER

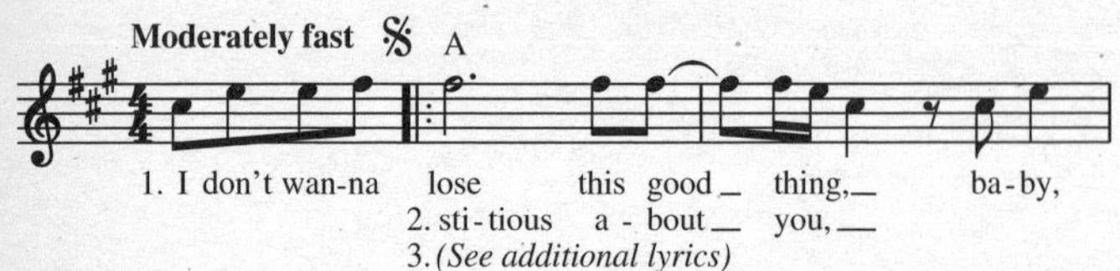
Moderately fast
A
1. I don't wan-na lose this good thing, ba-by,
2. sti-tious a - bout you,
3. (See additional lyrics)

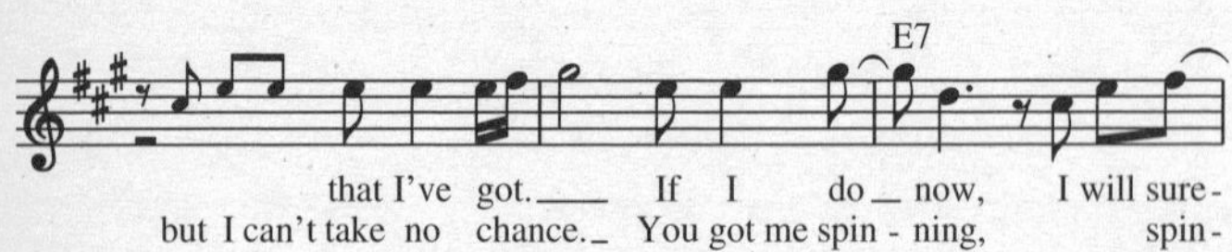
E7
that I've got. If I do now, I will sure-
but I can't take no chance. You got me spin - ning, spin-

- ly, I got to, I got to lose a lot.
- ning; ba-by; ba-by, I'm in a trance.
'Cause your love

A
is bet - ter than an - y love I know.

E
A
It's like thun - der, light - ning;

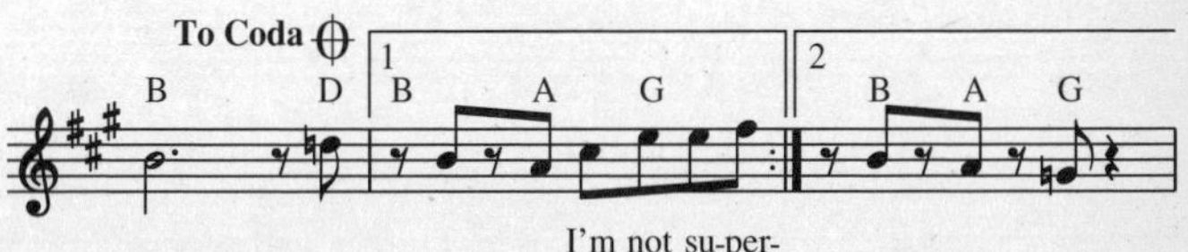

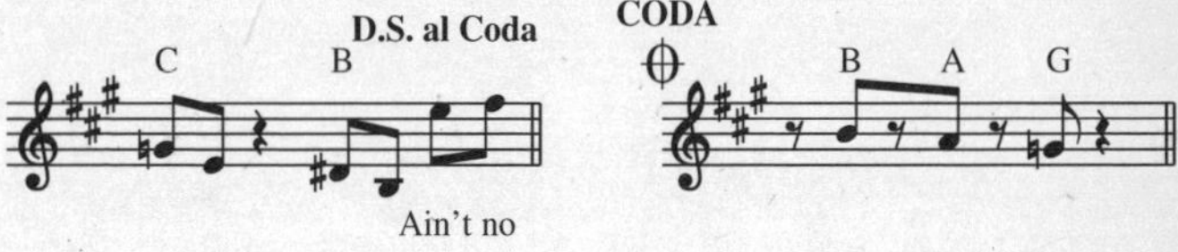

Additional Lyrics

3. Ain't no secret that a woman can feel my love come up.
You got me seeing, she really sees that, that I get enough.
Just one touch from you, baby, you know it means so much.
It's like thunder, lightning;
The way you love me is frightening,
I think I better knock, knock, knock, knock, knock on wood.

LAND OF A THOUSAND DANCES

Words and Music by
CHRIS KENNER

D
Ugh! Na na na na na ___ na na na na ___ na na na na na na na na na na. ___
Spoken: I need somebody to help me say it one
time. C'mon y'all, let's say it one more time.
Na na na na na ___ na na na na ___ na na na na na na na na na na ___ Ow!
1
Ugh!
D'you know I feel all right, huh! Feel pret-ty good y'all huh ___ ha!
2
Ow!
D
Repeat and Fade
Spoken: Baby have a party
Twisting with Lucy,
Roll over on your back,
do that Jerk.
with long tall Sally,
doing the Watusi.
I like it like that,
Watch me work, y'all.

LITTLE RED ROOSTER

Written by
WILLIE DIXON

Moderate Blues tempo
A7
1. I am a Lit-tle Red Roost - er, too la - zy to crow for day,
D7
I am a Lit-tle Red Roost-er,
A
E7
too la-zy to crow for day.
Keep ev-'ry-thing in the
D7
barn -yard
up - set in ev-ery way.
1.,2.
A7
3.
A7
2.,3. (See additional lyrics)

Additional Lyrics

2. The dogs begin to bark and the hounds begin to howl.
The dogs begin to bark and the hounds begin to howl.
Oh, watch out strange kin people, the Little Red Rooster is on the prowl.

3. If you see my little red rooster, please drive him home.
If you see my little red rooster, please drive him home.
There's been no peace in the barnyard since my Little Red Rooster's been gone.

LOVE AND HAPPINESS

Words and Music by AL GREEN
and MABON HODGES

B♭7
Gm
F
you real-ly feel good a-bout some-bod - y,
Gm
F
Gm
F
with noth - ing wrong.
Be-ing in
D♭ Cm
B♭
D♭ Cm
B♭
love with some-one,
yeah,
yeah.
D♭ Cm B♭
E♭7
D7
Gm
Oh ba - by,
love and hap - pi -
E♭7
D7
Gm
ness.
(Love and hap - pi-ness.)
Love and hap - pi -
Gm
ness.
(Love and hap - pi-ness.)
(Instrumental)
1

2
Eb7 D7 Gm
Help me sing: love and hap - pi -
Eb7 D7 Gm
ness.
(Love and hap - pi-ness.)
Love and hap - pi -
ness.
(Love and hap - pi - ness.)
You got to be
Bb
good to me, and I'll be
Bb7
good to you. We'll
3
Gm F Gm F
be to-geth - er. yeah; see each
Gm F Db Cm Bb
oth - er, walk a - way with vic - to - ry, yeah.
Db Cm Bb Db Cm Bb
Yeah. Oh ba - by,

Eb7
D7
Gm
love _ and hap - pi - ness.
(Love and hap - pi - ness.)
Eb7
D7
Gm
Love ___ and hap - pi -
ness.
(Love and hap - pi - ness.)
Hey, hey, __ hey. __
Make you do right, yeah. __
ear - ly, oh. ___
(See additional lyrics)
Love - 'll make you do wrong, ___ yeah._
Make you stay out all night_long.
1-5
6
Make you come home
Pow - er of love.
(Love and hap - pi -

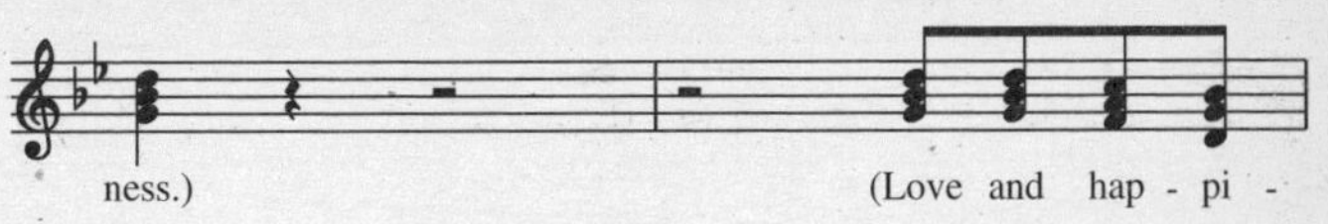
ness.)
(Love and hap - pi -

ness.)
(Love and hap - pi -
Sweet love will make you

ness.)
wan - na dance and

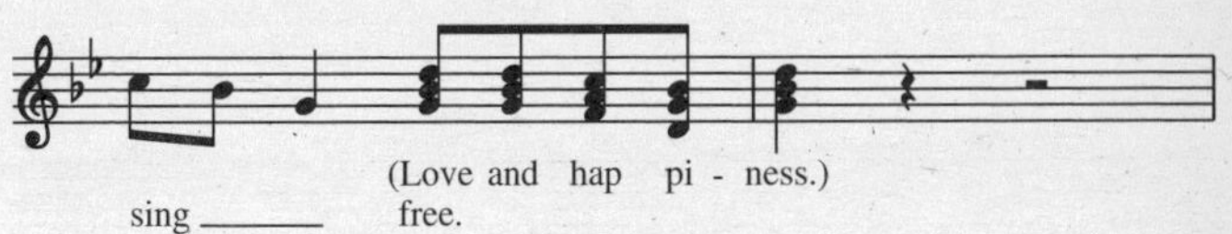
(Love and hap pi - ness.)
sing free.

Eb7 D7 Gm
Make you wan - na dance.

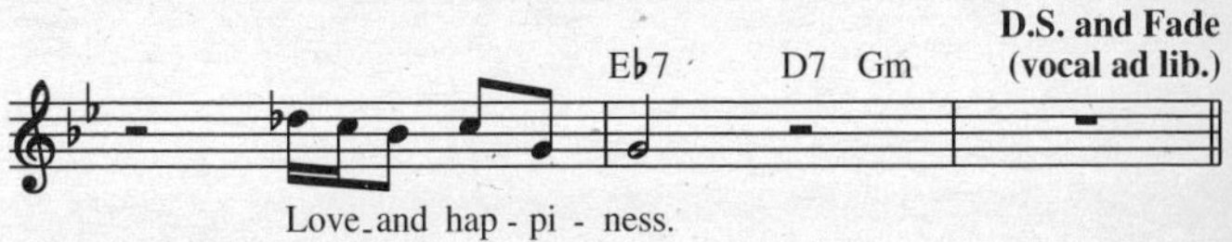
D.S. and Fade
(vocal ad lib.)
Eb7 D7 Gm
Love and hap - pi - ness.

Additional Lyrics

Wait a minute,
Let me tell you 'bout the power,
The power of love; hey, hey, hey.
Power... power...
Make you do right...
Love'll make you do wrong.

LONELY AVENUE

Words and Music by
DOC POMUS

Slowly
F7
Now my room has got two win - dows ___ but the
cov - ers they feel like lead ___ and my
been so sad and lone - some ___
sun - shine nev - er comes thru. ___ you know it's
pil - low it feels ___ like stone. ___ Well, ___ I've
since you've left ___ this town. ___ If I could
al - ways dark and drear - y ___ since I
tossed and turned so ev - 'ry night. ___ I'm not
beg or bor - row the mon - ey, child, I would
broke off, ba - by, with you! ___
used to be - ing a - lone! ___
to a - high - way bound! ___
I live on a
B♭7
lone - ly av - e - nue; ___ my lit - tle

girl would - n't say, "I do." Well, I
F7
feel so sad and blue and it's
all be - cause of you. I could
C7
cry, I could cry, I could cry. I could
B♭7
die, I could die, I could die, be - cause I live on a
F7
lone - ly av - e - nue,
1,2
lone-ly av - e - nue.
Now my
Now I've
3
F9
lone-ly av - e - nue.

LONELY TEARDROPS

Words and Music by BERRY GORDY, GWEN GORDY FUQUA and TYRAN CARLO

2
C C9 F
Just give me an - oth - er
Fm
chance for our ro - mance. Come on and
C E7
tell me that one day you'll re - turn,
F
'cause ev - 'ry day that you've
G7
been gone a - way, you'll know how my heart does
D.C. al Coda
C C9
noth - ing but burn. Cry - in'
CODA
C Am
Hey. Say it right now, ba - by.
C
Come on, come on.

MARY ANN

Words and Music by
RAY CHARLES

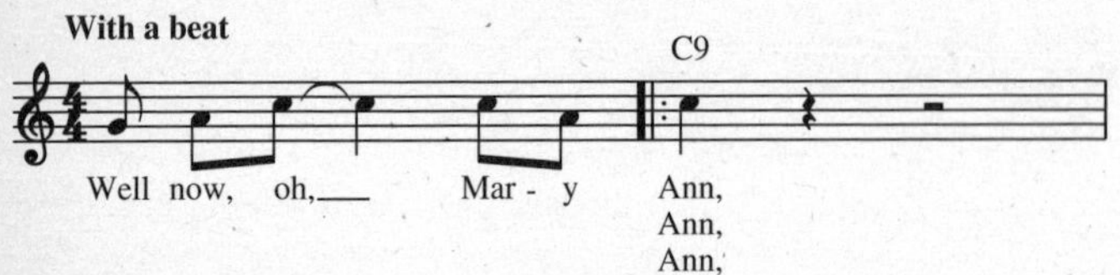
With a beat
C9
Well now, oh, Mar - y Ann,
Ann,
Ann,

you know you sure look fine.
I said, ba - by don't you know?
can I take you home to - night?

Well now, oh,
Oh,
Oh,

F9
ba - by,
ba - by,
ba - by,

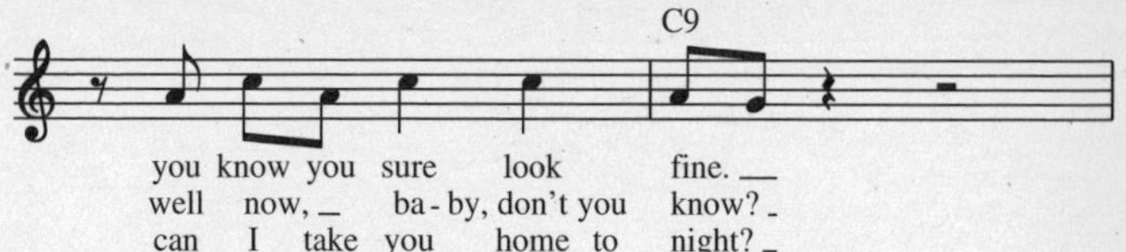
C9
you know you sure look fine. __
well now, _ ba - by, don't you know? _
can I take you home to night? _

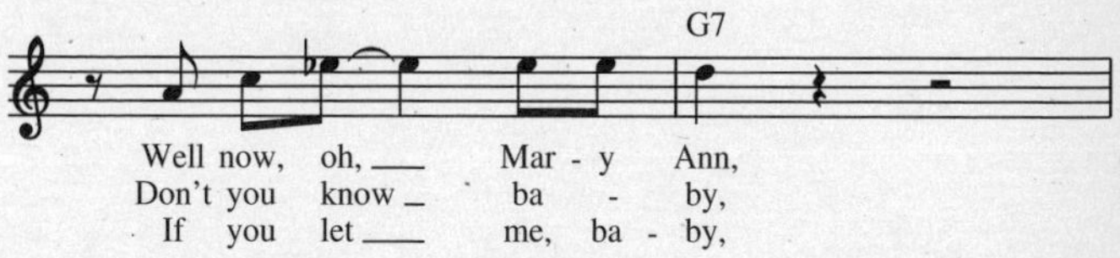
G7
Well now, oh, ___ Mar - y Ann,
Don't you know _ ba - by,
If you let ___ me, ba - by,

F7
I could love you all the time. __
that I love you so? ___
I'll make ev - 'ry - thing all right. __

1,2
C9
Well now, oh, ___ Mar - y
Oh, ___________ Mar - y

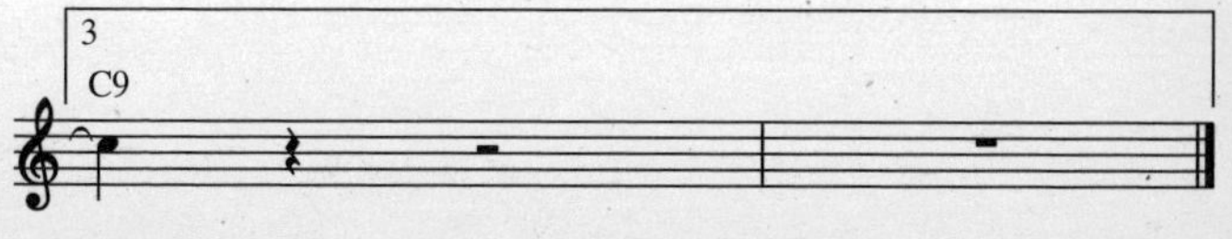
3
C9

MR. PITIFUL

Words and Music by OTIS REDDING
and STEVE CROPPER

Fast Rock
C
C7 F/C C
They call me Mis - ter Pit - i - ful;
2.(See additional lyrics)

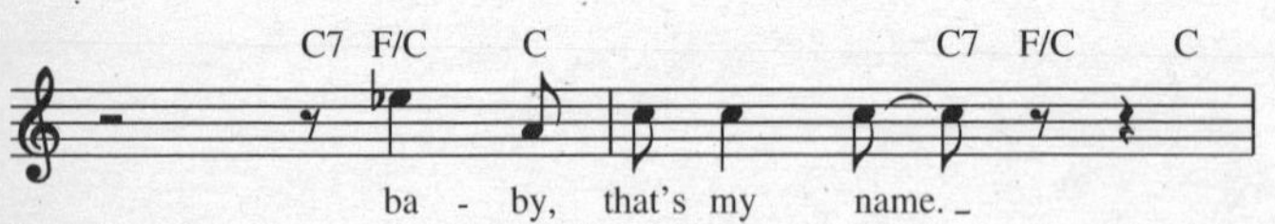
C7 F/C C
C7 F/C C
ba - by, that's my name.

C7 F/C C
C7 F/C C
They call me Mis - ter Pit - i - ful;

G
G7 C/G G
that's how I got my fame.

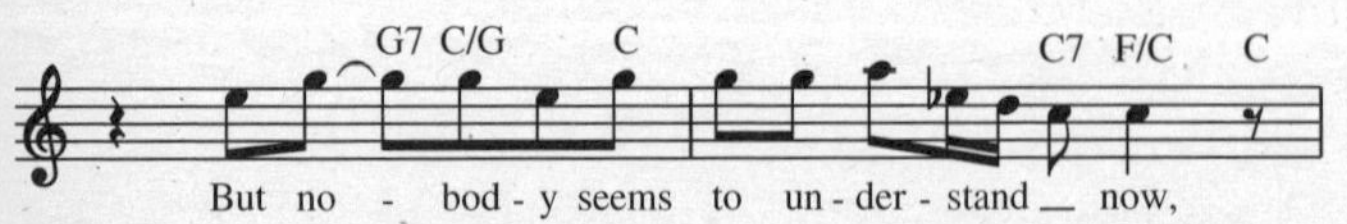
G7 C/G C
C7 F/C C
But no - bod - y seems to un - der - stand now,

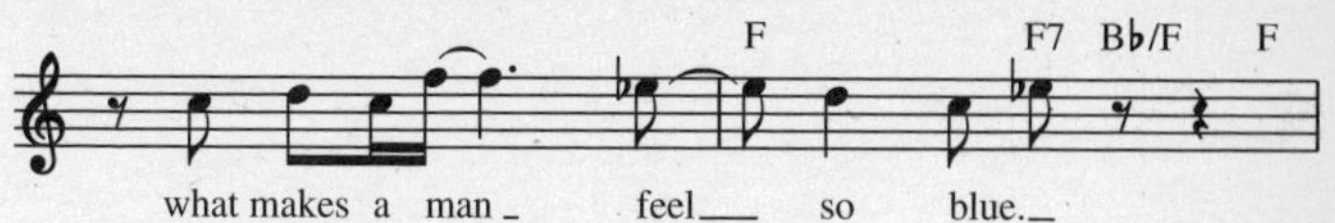
F
F7 B♭/F F
what makes a man feel so blue.

F7 B♭/F C
C7 F/C G
Oh, they call me Mis - ter Pit - i - ful

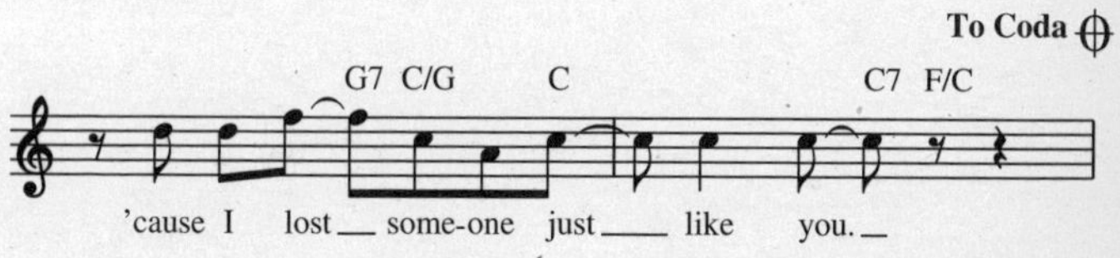
To Coda
G7 C/G C
C7 F/C
'cause I lost some-one just like you.

1
C N.C.
2
C N.C.
2. They call me Mis - ter.
(Instrumental)

C

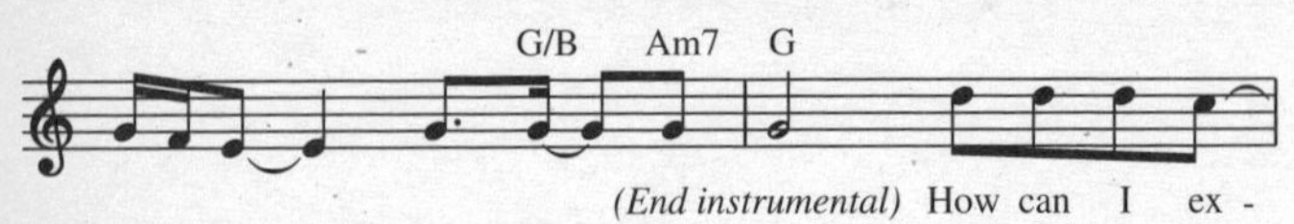

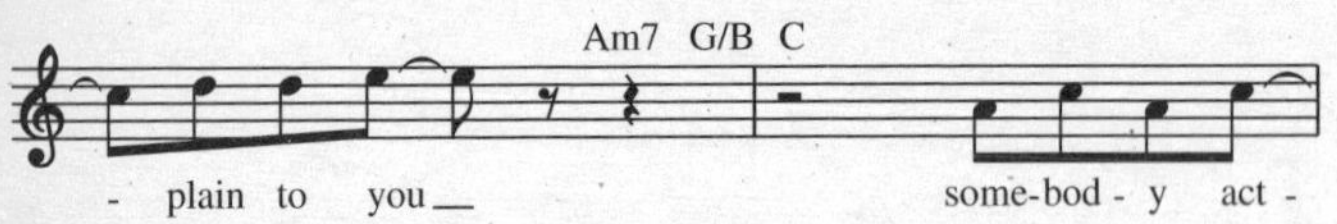

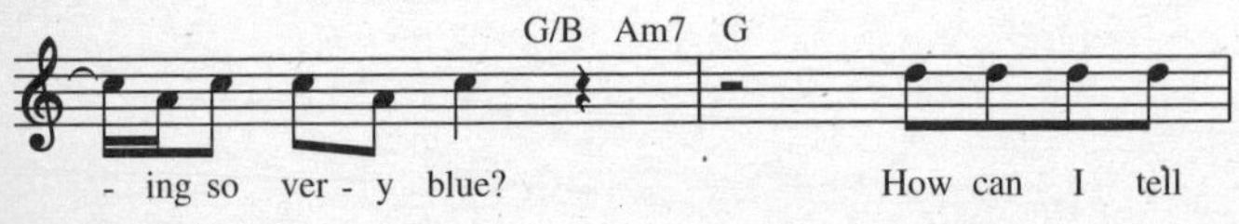

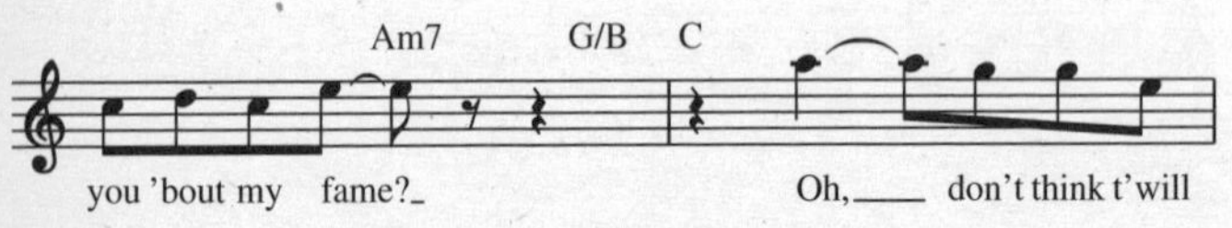

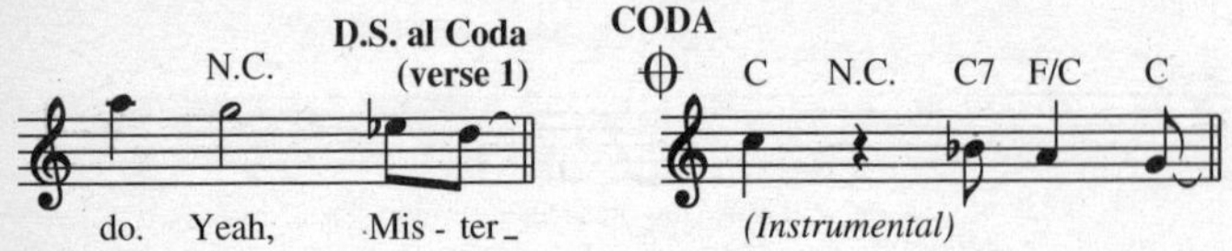

Additional Lyrics

2. They call me Mr. Pitiful; yes, everybody knows, now.
   They call me Mr. Pitiful most every place I go.
   But nobody seems to understand, now,
   what makes a man sing such a sad song,
   When he lost everything, when he lost everything he had.

MUSTANG SALLY

Words and Music by
BONNY RICE

Moderate Blues Rock

C7
Mus-tang Sal-ly. Think you bet-ter

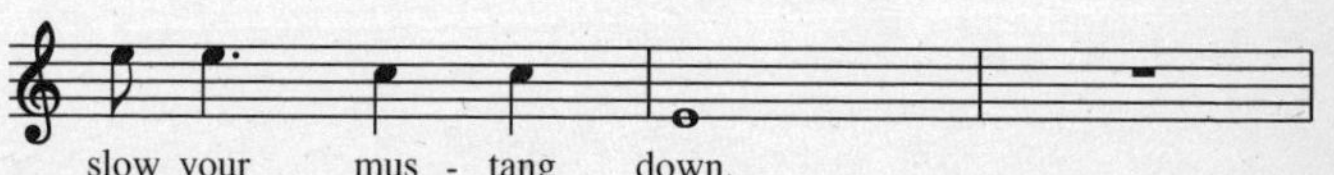
slow your mus - tang down.

F7
Mus-tang Sal - ly.

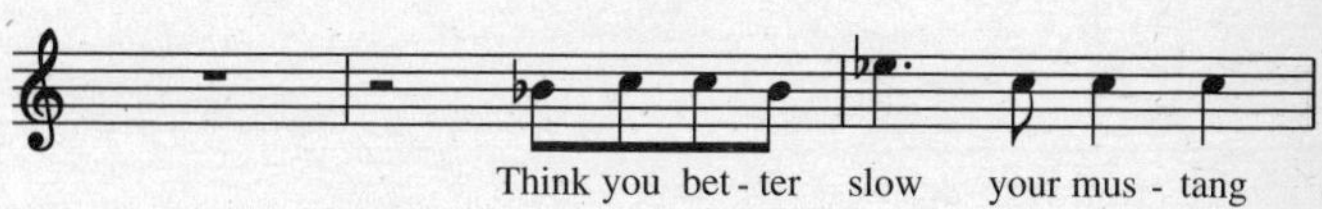
Think you bet - ter slow your mus - tang

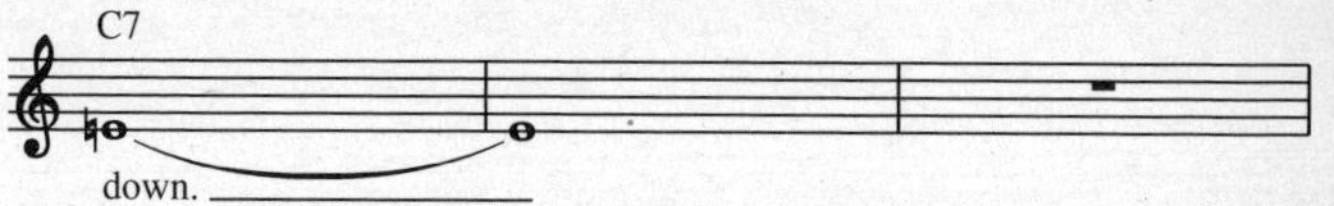
C7
down.

G7
You been run-ing all o - ver the town now.

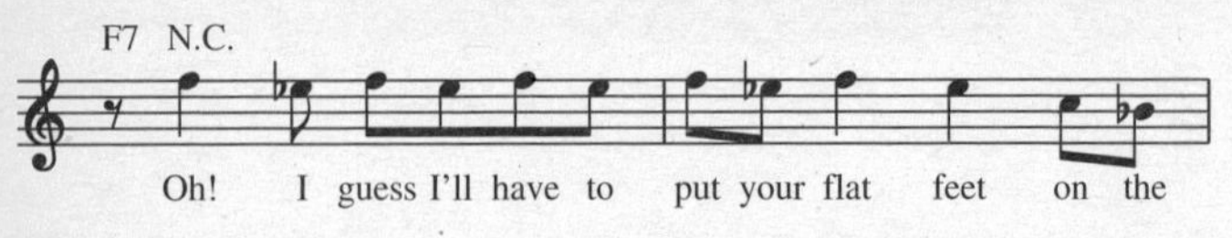
F7 N.C.
Oh! I guess I'll have to put your flat feet on the

To Coda

C7
G7
ground.

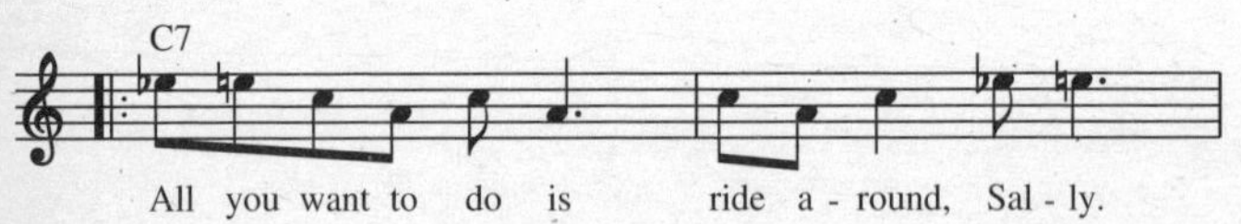
C7
All you want to do is ride a - round, Sal - ly.

F7
Ride, Sal - ly ride.
All you want to do is

ride a-round, Sal - ly. Ride, Sal - ly ride.

C7
All you want to do is ride a - round, Sal - ly.

G7
Ride, Sal - ly ride. One of these ear - ly

F7 N.C.
morn-ings, Oh, you gon-na be wip-ing your weep - ing

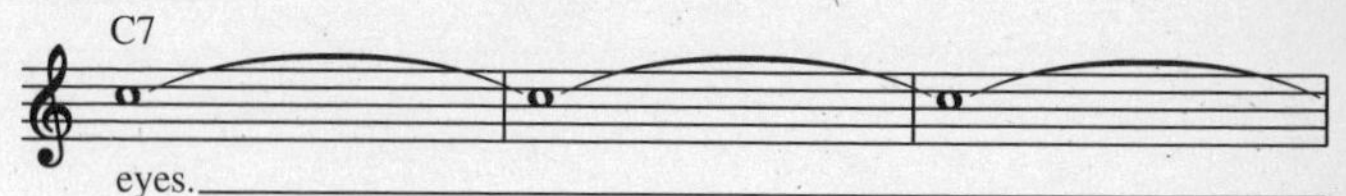
C7
eyes.

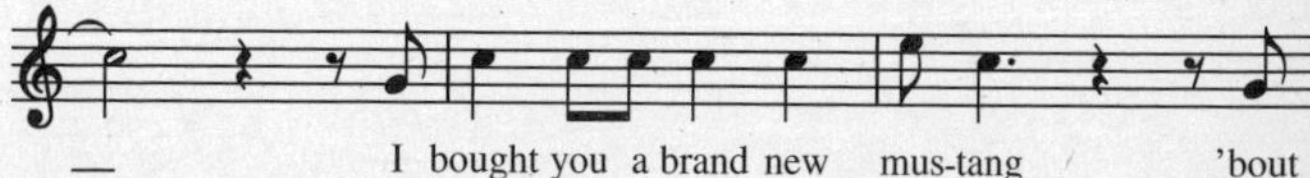
I bought you a brand new mus-tang 'bout

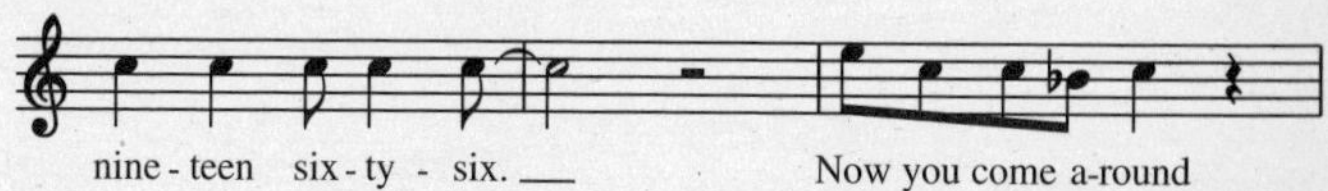
nine - teen six - ty - six.
Now you come a-round

sig - ni - fy-ing a wom-an, you don't wan - na let me ride.

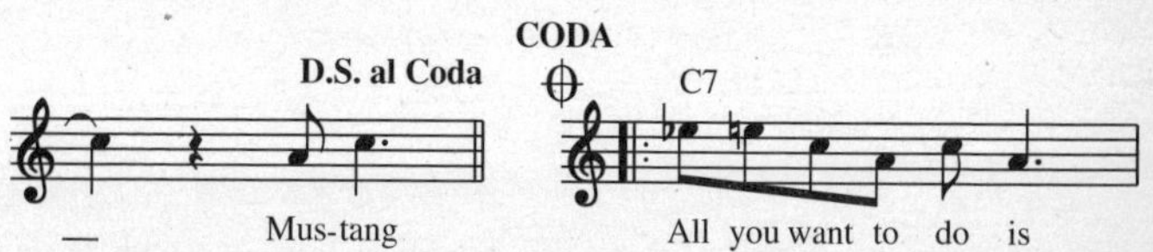
D.S. al Coda
CODA
C7
Mus-tang
All you want to do is

Repeat and Fade
ride a-round, Sal-ly. Ride, Sal - ly ride.

MY GIRL

Words and Music by WILLIAM "SMOKEY" ROBINSON
and RONALD WHITE

Slowly
F
B♭
I've got sun - shine
on a cloud - y

F
B♭
F
day;
When it's cold out - side,

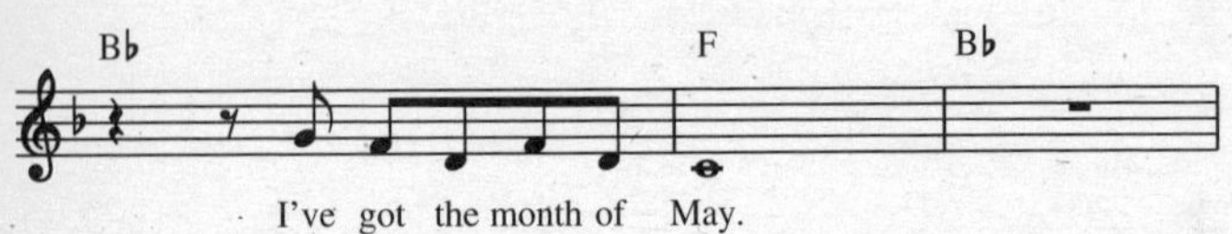
B♭
F
B♭
I've got the month of May.

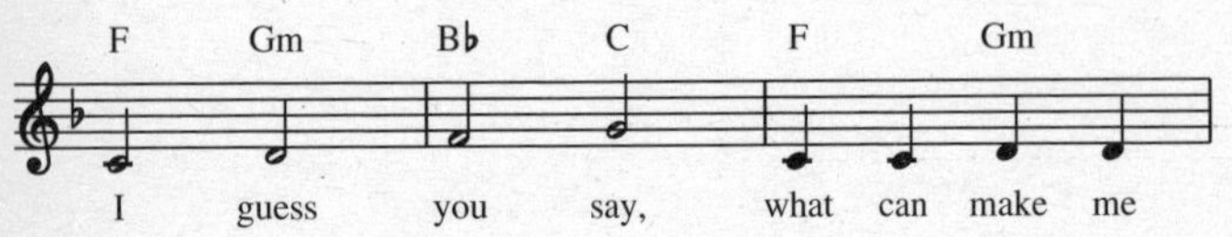
F
Gm
B♭
C
F
Gm
I guess you say, what can make me

B♭
C
F
feel this way? My girl,
talk-ing 'bout

B♭
C7
3
my
girl.
I've got

F
B♭
F
so much hon-ey, the bees en-vy me;

B♭
F
I've got a sweet-er song

B♭
F
B♭
than the birds in the tree.
Well,

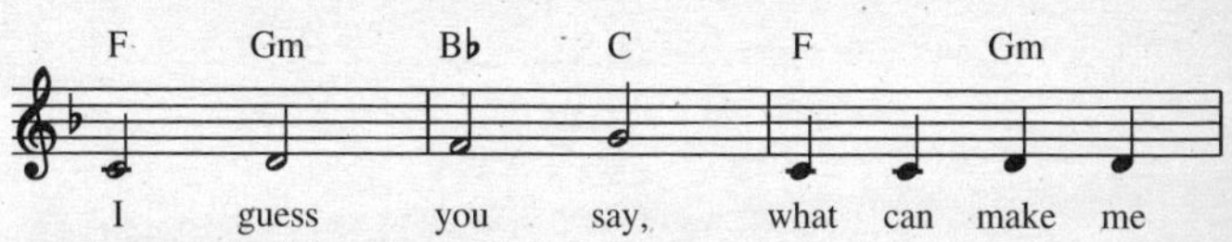
F Gm B♭ C F Gm
I guess you say, what can make me

B♭ C F
feel this way? My girl,
talk-ing 'bout

B♭
C7
3
my girl.
I don't

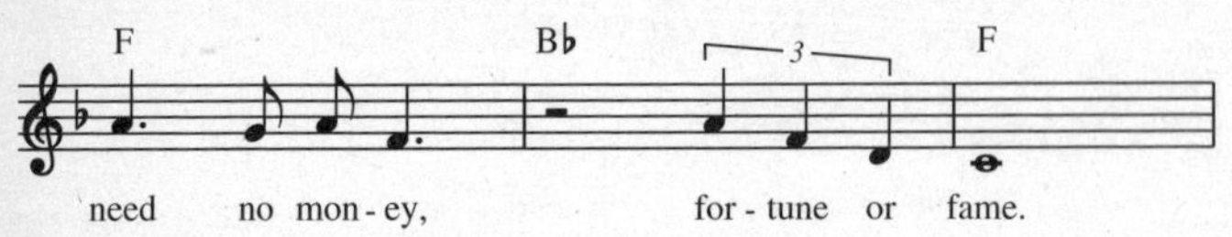
F
B♭
3
F
need no mon - ey,
for - tune or fame.

B♭
3
F
I've got all the rich - es, ba - by,

B♭
F
B♭
one man can claim.
Well,

F
Gm
B♭
C
F
Gm
I guess you say, what can make me

B♭
C
F
feel this way? My girl,
talk-ing 'bout

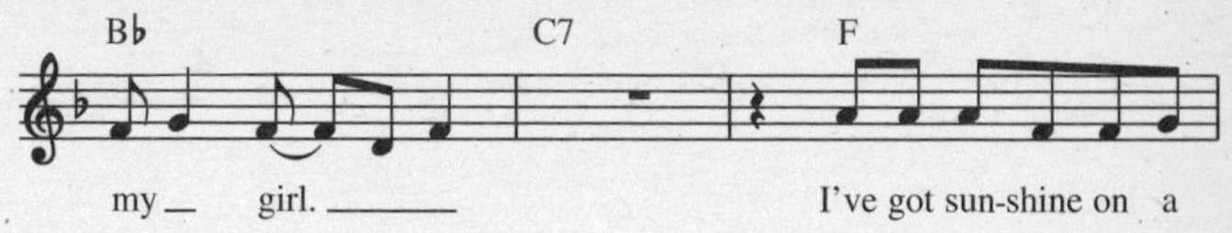
B♭
C7
F
my girl.
I've got sun-shine on a

Gm
cloud - y day with my girl;
I've

C7
F
e - ven got the month of May with my girl.

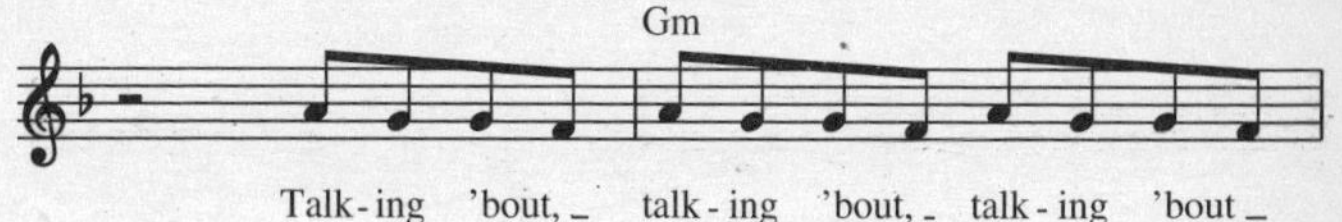
Gm
Talk-ing 'bout, talk-ing 'bout, talk-ing 'bout

C7
F
my girl.
Woo!
My girl.

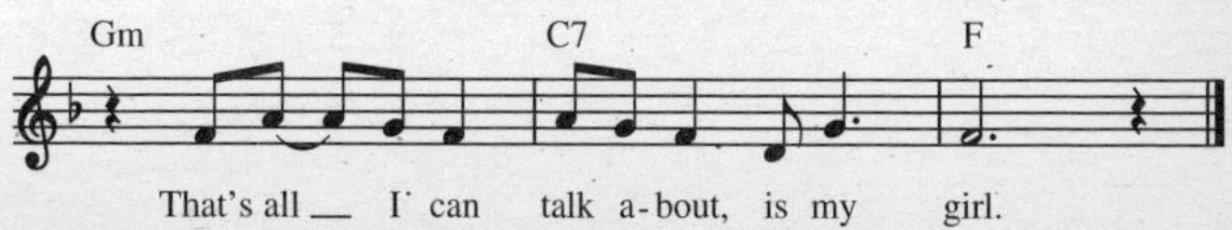
Gm
C7
F
That's all I can talk a-bout, is my girl.

(You Make Me Feel Like)
A NATURAL WOMAN

Words and Music by GERRY GOFFIN, CAROLE KING and JERRY WEXLER

C♯m7
Bm7
C♯m7
met you, life was so un - kind.
doubt-ful of what I'm liv - ing for, 'cause
Bm7
C♯m7
Your love was the key to my peace of
if I make you hap - py I don't need to do
Dmaj7
Bm7/E
A
3
mind,
more,
'cause you make me feel,
D
A
3
D
you make me feel,
You Make Me
A D A/C♯ A D A/C♯ Bm7 Bm7/E
Feel Like A Nat - u - ral Wom-an.
A
G/A
Oh, ba - by, what you've done to me! (What you've
D
A
done to me!)
You make me
G/A
feel so good in-side. (Good in - side.)

Dmaj7 Am7/D
And I just want to be
D
(want to be) close to you. You
A/C# Bm7
make me feel so a - live! You
Bm7/E A Dmaj7
make me feel, you make me
A Dmaj7
feel, You Make Me
1, 2
A D A/C# A D A/C# Bm7
Feel Like A Nat - u - ral, nat - u - ral
3
Bm7/E Bm7
wom - an. You make me Wom - an, a
Bm7/E A D A/C# Bm7 A
nat - u - ral wom-an.

ONE MINT JULEP

Words and Music by
RUDOLPH TOOMBS

Slow Rock
D
G9
One ear - ly morn - in' as I was walk - in',
I don't re - mem - ber just how it start - ed,
D
G9
I met a wom - an and start - ed talk - in'.
but all I know is, we should have part - ed.
D
G9
Went in a tav - ern to get a few nips.
I stole a kiss, and then an - oth - er.
D
G9
But all I had was a mint ju - lep.
I did - n't mean to take it fur - ther.
A7
Gmaj9
One mint ju - lep was the cause of it all.
1
D
2
D

F#7
The lights were burn - ing low

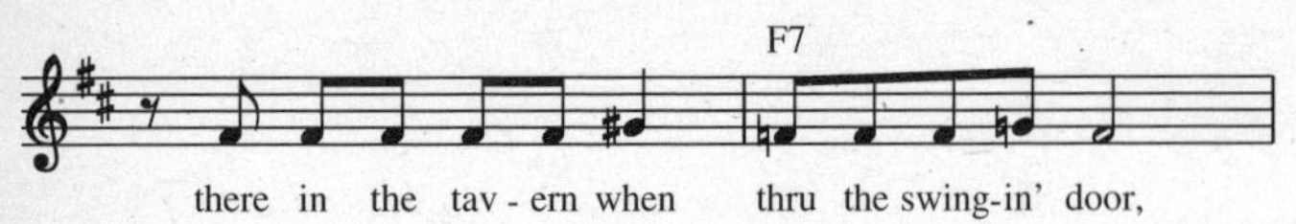
F7
there in the tav - ern when thru the swing-in' door,

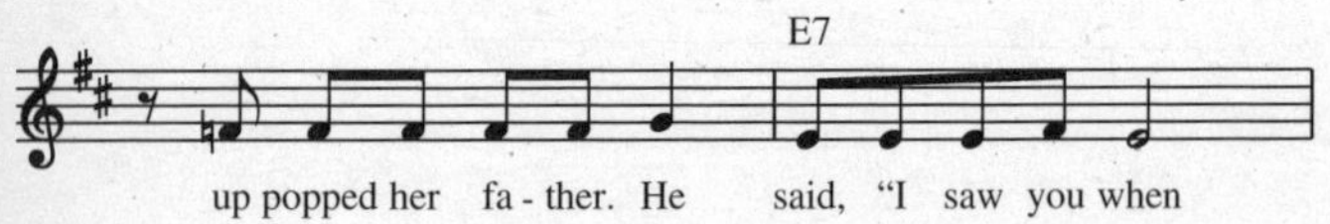
E7
up popped her fa - ther. He said, "I saw you when

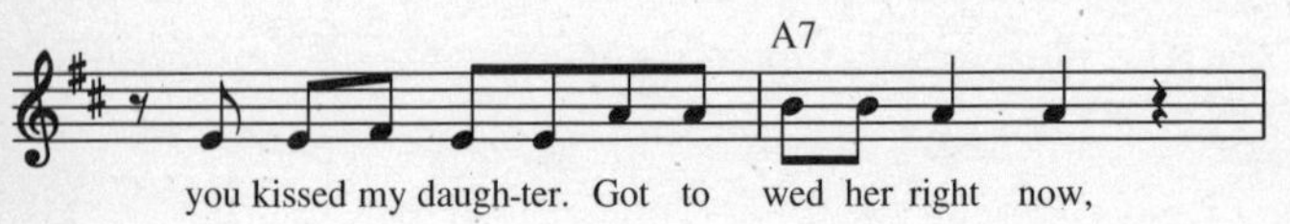
A7
you kissed my daugh-ter. Got to wed her right now,

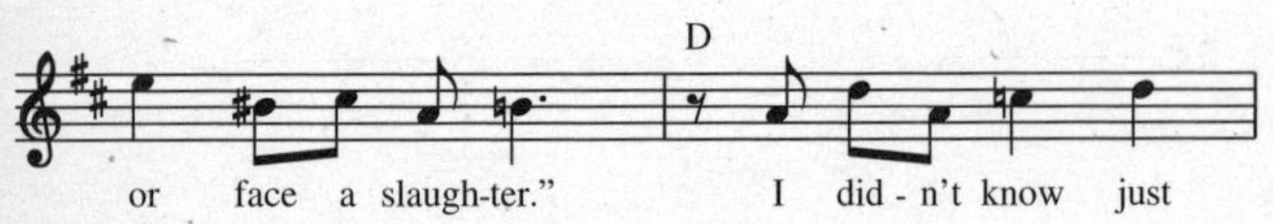
D
or face a slaugh-ter." I did - n't know just

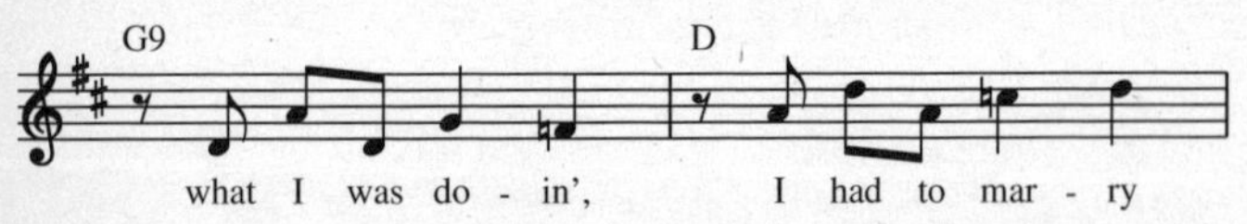
G9
D
what I was do - in', I had to mar - ry

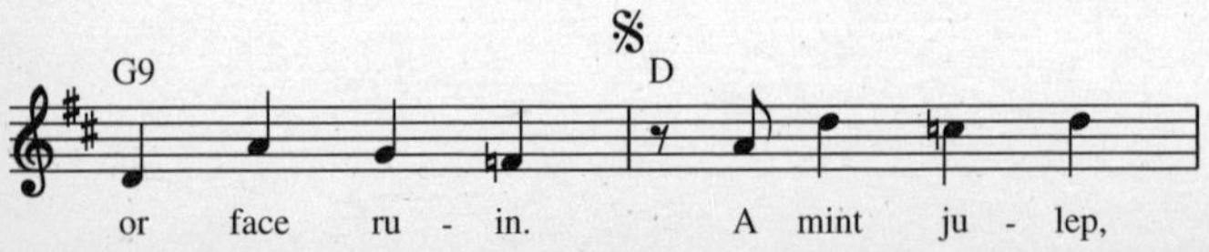
G9
D
or face ru - in. A mint ju - lep,

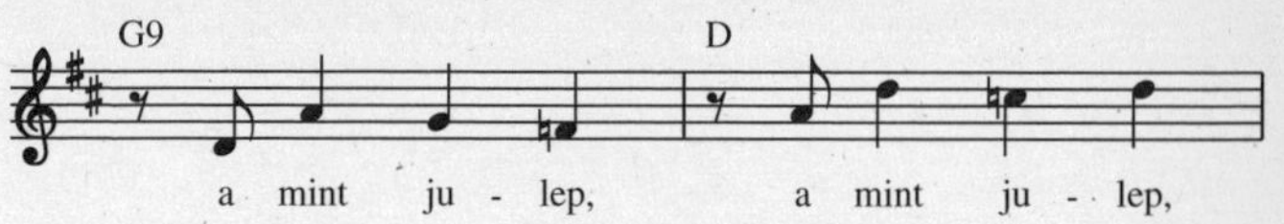
G9
D
a mint ju - lep, a mint ju - lep,

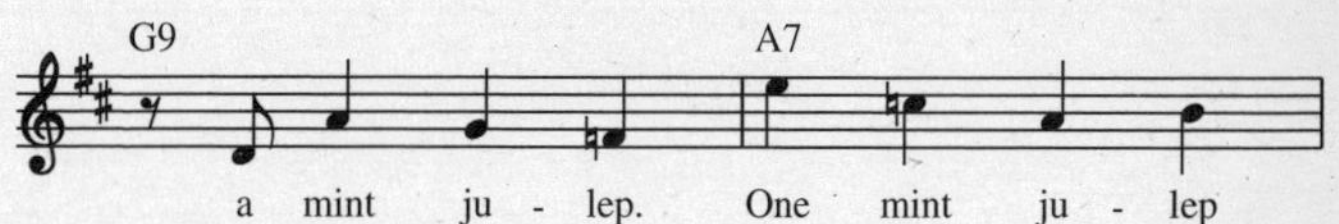
G9
A7
a mint ju - lep. One mint ju - lep

Gmaj9
D
Fine
was the cause of it all. I

F#7
don't want to bore you with my trou - ble, but from

F7
now on I'll be think - ing dou - ble. I'll

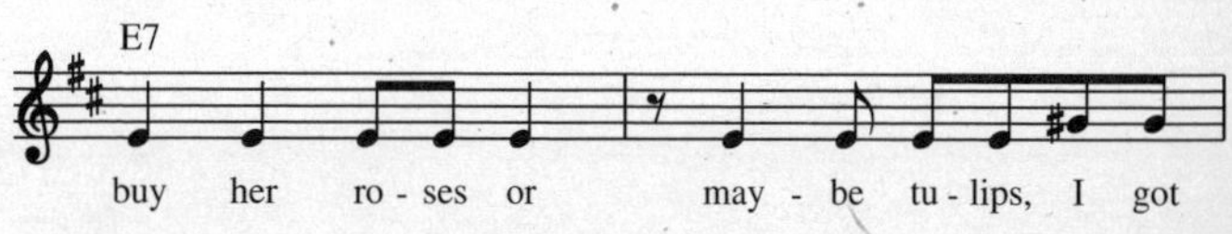
E7
buy her ro - ses or may - be tu - lips, I got

A7
D.S. al Fine
too much trou - ble from buy - ing ju - leps.

PAIN IN MY HEART

Words and Music by
NAOMI NEVILLE

Moderate Blues Ballad

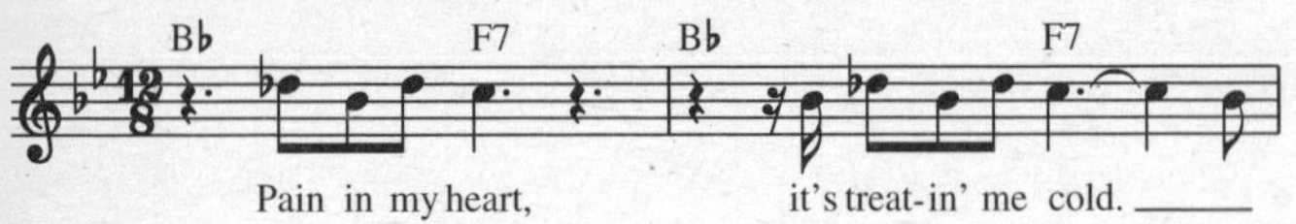
B♭
F7
B♭
F7
Pain in my heart,
it's treat-in' me cold.

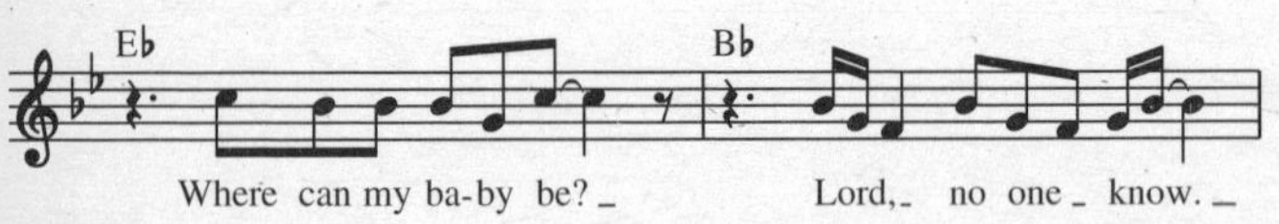
E♭
B♭
Where can my ba-by be?
Lord, no one know.

F7
B♭
F7
Pain in my heart,
just won't let me sleep.

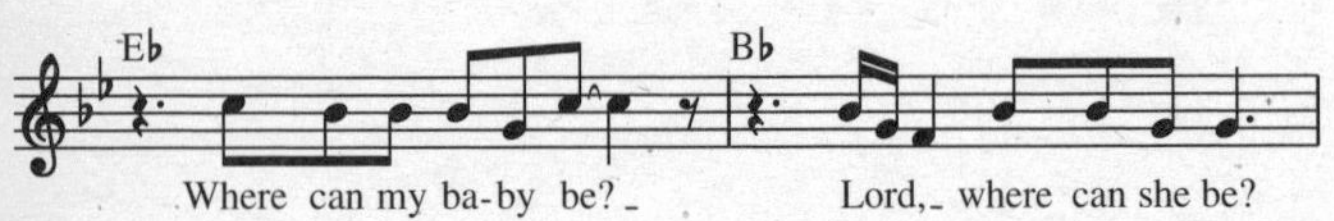
E♭
B♭
Where can my ba-by be?
Lord, where can she be?

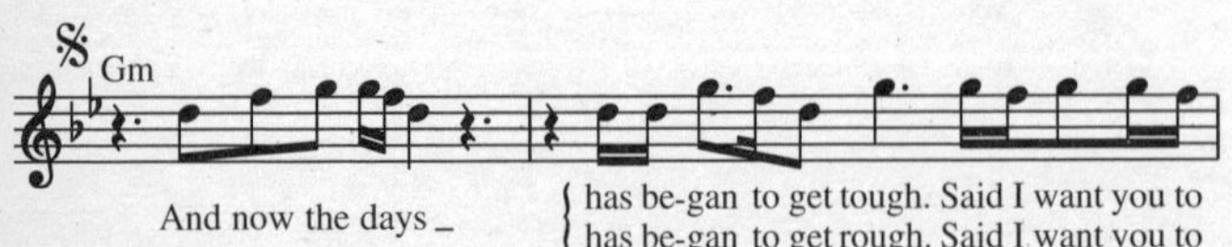
Gm
And now the days
has be-gan to get tough. Said I want you to
has be-gan to get rough. Said I want you to

B♭
N.C.
come back, come back, come back, ba - by.
love me, love me, love me, ba - by.

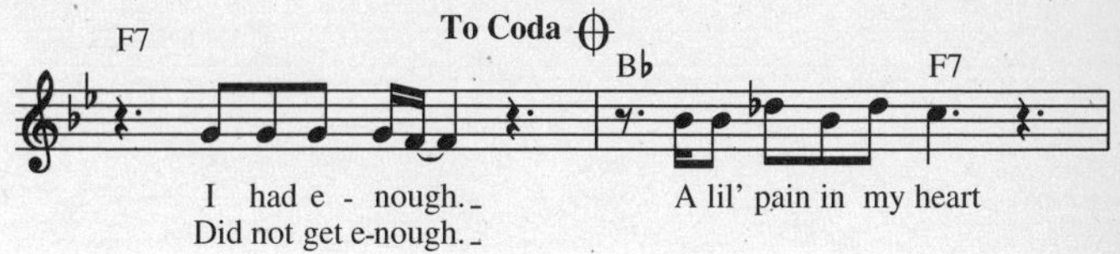
F7
To Coda
B♭
F7
I had e - nough.
Did not get e-nough.
A lil' pain in my heart

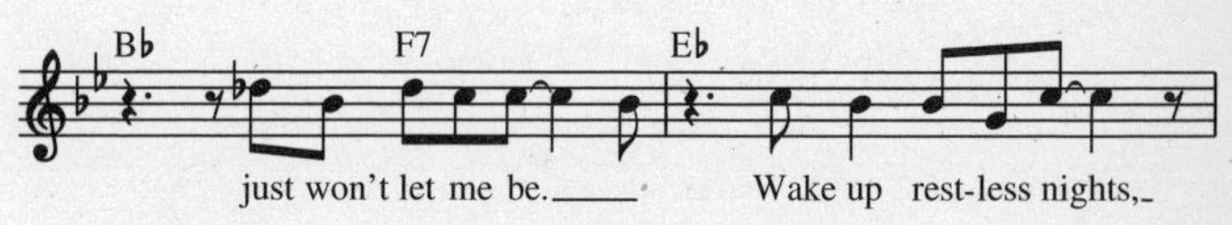
B♭
F7
E♭
just won't let me be.
Wake up rest-less nights,

B♭
F7
Lord, and I can't e - ven sleep.

B♭
F7
B♭
D.S. al Coda
(Instrumental)

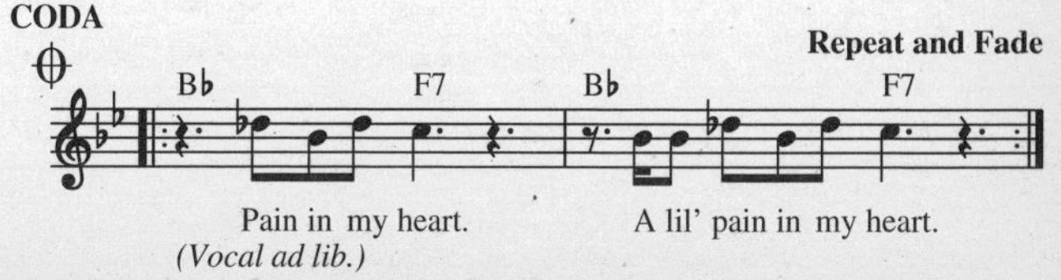
CODA
Repeat and Fade
B♭
F7
B♭
F7
Pain in my heart.
A lil' pain in my heart.
(Vocal ad lib.)

PAPA'S GOT A BRAND NEW BAG

Words and Music by
JAMES BROWN

1
B9
Come here
2
B9
He's do-in' the
E9
jerk; he's do - in' the
fly. Don't play him cheap 'cause you know he's too shy.
He's do - in' the
mon-key, the mashed po - ta-toes, jump back Jack,
see you la - ter al - li - ga - tor.
D.S. al Coda
B7
Come here
CODA
B9

PICK UP THE PIECES

Words and Music by JAMES HAMISH STUART,
ALAN GORRIE, ROGER BALL, ROBBIE McINTOSH,
OWEN McINTYRE and MALCOLM DUNCAN

Fm7
1
2
B♭7sus
C7♯5(♯9)
Fm7

Bb7
Fm7
To Coda
Bb7
C7#5(#9)
Pick up the piec-es, uh huh,

pick up the piec-es, oh, yeah. Pick up the piec-es, yeah,
CODA
D.S. al Coda
B♭7sus
pick up the piec-es.
C7♯5(♯9)
Fm7
(Sung:) Pick up the piec - es.
Pick up the piec - es.
1
2
Pick up the

PLEASE ACCEPT MY LOVE

Words and Music by B.B. KING
and SAUL BIHARI

Moderately
N.C.
G
I don't e - ven know your name,

D7
but I love you just the same.

Dar - ling, let me hold your hand

G
till I make you un - der - stand.

N.C.
If you on - ly, on - ly

G
knew just how much I

D7
love you.
Lov-ing you the way

that I do,
you'd take to - night to

G
N.C.
love me too.
And like the pic - ture on the

C
wall,
please don't

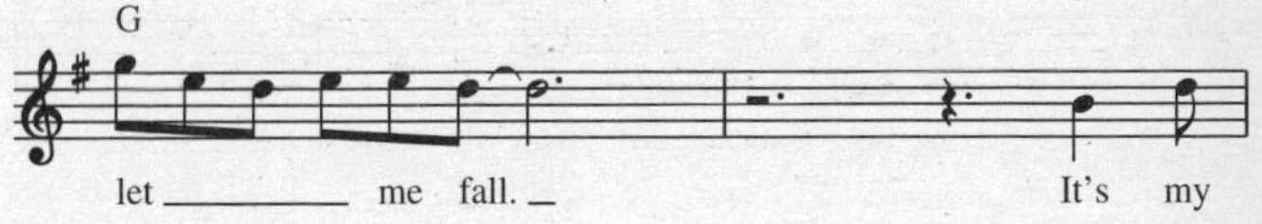
G
let me fall.
It's my

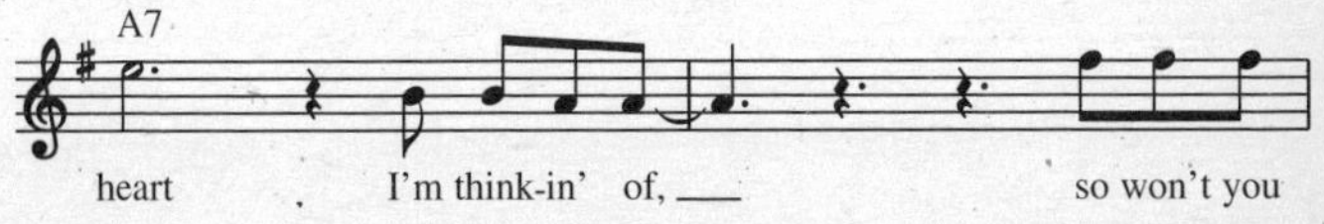
A7
heart I'm think-in' of,
so won't you

D7
N.C.
D7
please, please ac - cept my

N.C.
G
love. If you let me be _ your slave, ___
your love ___ I'll cher - ish to my
4
D7
grave. ___
And if you die _ be -
fore I do, ___
1
I'd end my life ___ to be _
G
N.C.
___ with you. ___
And like the pic - ture on the
2
N.C.
I'll end my life to be with
G G7/B C C#dim D7 N.C. F#7 G7
you. ___

RESPECT YOURSELF

Words and Music by MACK RICE
and LUTHER INGRAM

Moderately
Cm
If you dis - re - spect ev - 'ry - bod - y that you run in - to how in the world do you think ev - 'ry - bod - y s'posed to re - spect you?
walk - in' round think - in' that the world owes you some-thin' 'cause you're here you're go-ing out the world back-wards like you did when you first came here.
If you don't give a heck a - bout the man with the Bi - ble in his hand, just get out the way and let the gen - tle - man do his thing.
Keep talk-in' 'bout the pres - i - dent won't stop air pol - lu - tion, put your hand o'er your mouth when you cough; that'll help the so-lu -

tion.
You
You the kind of gen - tle man want ev - 'ry - thing your way.
cuss a - round wom - en - folk, you don't e - ven know their name,
Take the
Then you're
sheet off your face, boy, it's a brand new day.
dumb e - nough to think that 'll make you a big ole man.
Re - spect your - self,
re - spect your - self,
re - spect your - self,
re - spect your - self.

If you
G
don't re - spect your - self ain't no - bod - y
gon - na give a good, good hoot - e - nan - ny, boy! Re -
Cm
spect your - self, re -
spect your - self, re -
spect your - self, re -
1
spect your - self. If you're
2
Repeat and Fade
spect your - self. Re -

A RAINY NIGHT IN GEORGIA

Words and Music by
TONY JOE WHITE

Moderately
Ebmaj7
Ab
1. Hov-erin' by my suit-case, tryin' to find a warm place to
2. Ne - on signs a-flash-in', tax - i - cabs and busses pass-in'
3. (See additional lyrics)
Ebmaj7
spend the night; A
through the night; The
Ab
heav - y rain a-fall - in'; Seems I hear your voice call - in'
dis - tant moan - in' of a train Seems to play a sad re - frain
Ebmaj7
Chorus
Cm
"It's all right."
to the night;
A rain - y night In
Gm
Cm
Geor - gia, A rain - y night In

Additional Lyrics

3. I find me a place in a box car,
So I takc out my guitar to pass some time;
Late at night when it's hard to rest,
I hold your picture to my chest, and I'm all right;
Chorus

RESPECT

Words and Music by
OTIS REDDING

F
G
in re - turn, hon - ey, is to give me
so here's my mon - ey. All I want you to do for me
F
my pro - per re - spect
is give me some here
when you get
C
F
home. Yeah, ba - by, when you get
C7
home. (Just a lit - tle bit.
F
C7
Just a lit - tle bit.) R - E - S - P - E - C - T,
F
find out what it means to me,
C7
F
R - E - S - P - E - C - T, take out T - C - P.
Repeat and Fade
C7
F
A lit - tle re - spect.

A ROSE IS STILL A ROSE

Words and Music by LAURYN HILL, EDIE BRICKELL, KENNETH WITHROW, JOHN BUSH, JOHN HOUSER and ALAN ALY

(contains a sample of "What I Am")

B♭
A♭
She nev - er knew what hit her,
When she looks in the mir - ror
G♭
yeah,
B♭
steal her hon - ey then for - get her.
she's cry-ing. You can't hear her.
A♭
Now the rose is strong
gone
and she wears
A♭/D♭
G♭
G♭/C♭
a thong try - ing to for-get a-bout
B♭
Gm
you, 'cause a rose
Dm7
Cm7
Dm7
is still a rose.
Gm
Dm7
Cm7
Ba - by girl, you're still a flow - er.
Dm7
Gm
He can't leave you and then take

Dm7 Cm7 Dm7
you, make you and then break you.
1
Gm Dm7 To Coda Cm7
Dar - ling, you hold the pow - er.
Ba - by girl,
Dar - ling,
2
Dm7 Cm7 Dm7 D.S. al Coda
Now be - er. See, a
CODA
Cm7 Dm7 E♭maj7 Dm7
er. Let your life here
Cm7
in the sun - shine, not the dark - ness of
Dm7 E♭maj7 Dm7
your sor - row. You may feel you lost
Cm7
to - day, but new love will come
Dm7 E♭maj7 Dm7
to - mor - row. Don't be - lieve that life
Cm7
is o - ver just be - cause your man

Dm7
Eb maj7
Dm7
is gone. God, love your-self
Cm7
N.C.
e-nough to know that with-out him your life
Gm
Dm7
goes on. With-out him your life goes on.
Cm7
Dm7
Gm
With-out him your life goes on 'cause a rose
Dm7
Cm7
Dm7
is still a rose.
Gm
Dm7
Cm7
Ba-by girl, you're still a flow-er.
Dm7
Gm
Dm7
He can't leave you and then take you,
Cm7
Dm7
Gm
make you and then break you.
Ba-by girl,
Dar-ling,
Repeat and Fade
Dm7
Cm7
Dm7
you hold the pow-er.
See, a

SEE SAW

Words and Music by STEVE CROPPER
and DON COVAY

Moderate R&B
C7
Some-times you love me like a good man ought - a.
Some-times you hurt me so bad
my tears run like wa - ter.
You get me out
right be - fore your friends,
then you kiss on me, ba - by, un - til we're a - lone a - gain.
(2nd time, 8va)
Your love is like a see - saw,

your love is like a see - saw, ba - by.
Your love is like a see - saw, go - in'
up, down all a - round like a
To Coda
see - saw. Some-times - you tell me you're
gon-na be my sweet can - dy man;
then, uh, some-times ba - by, don't know where I
3
stand. Lift me up
when I'm on the ground. But soon as I

get up, you send me tumb - lin'
D.S. al Coda
down. Now! Your love is like a
CODA
E7
When I kiss you, and I like it and I
Am
ask you to kiss me a - gain. When
D7
I reach for you you jump c(uh) - lean out - a - sight. You
G7
C7
change just like the wind! Your love is like a
see - saw, your love is like a
Repeat and Fade
see - saw, ba - by. Your love is like a

SEND ME SOME LOVIN'

Words and Music by JOHN MARASCALCO
and LEO PRICE

Moderately slow
A
Send me some lov - in',
pic - ture,
ooh, send it I pray.
oh, send it, my dear,
E
How can I love you
so I can hold it
when you're so far a - way?
and pre - tend you are near.
A
D
1
E9 N.C.
Oh, hon-ey, send me your
2
Can you send me your

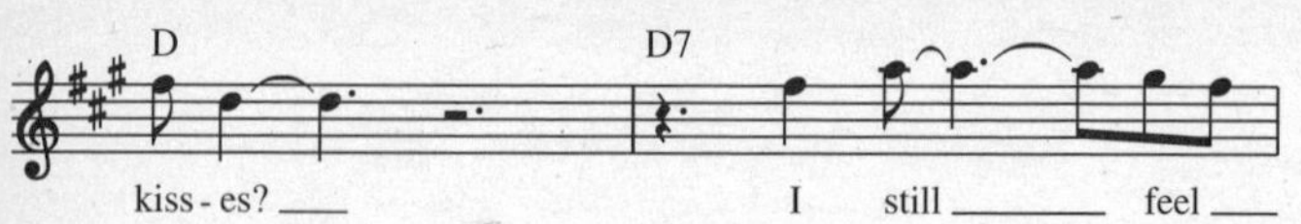
D
D7
kiss - es?
I still
feel

A
your touch.
And oh,
I need

B7
you
so bad - ly.

E7
I want you so much.

N.C.
A
My days are so lone - ly.

Oh, my nights are so

E
blue.
I'm here and I'm long -

E7
- in'
A D
and I'm _ a-wait-in' for you. I
E A
want you to send me some lov-in', ___
pic-ture, ___
E
send it, I pray. ___
send it, my dear, ___
How can I love you ___
so I can hold it ___
A
when you're so far a - way? ___
and pre-tend you are near. ___
1
2
Repeat and Fade
(Verse 1)
E7
E7
Send me your
Send me your

THEME FROM "SHAFT"

Words and Music by
ISAAC HAYES

Fmaj9
3
Em7
G
Fmaj9
Spoken: Who's the black private dick

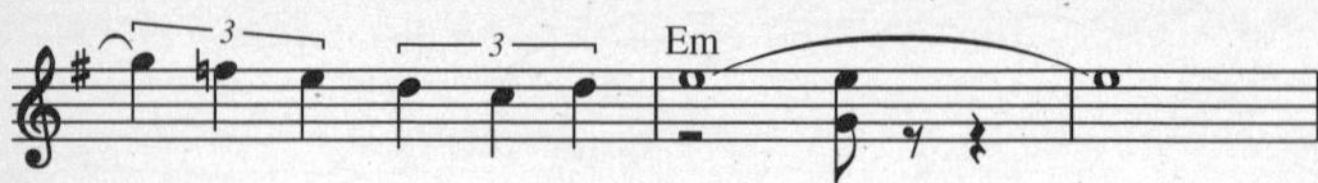
Em
that's a sex machine to all the chicks? (Shaft!)

Fmaj9
Em
Fmaj9
Sung:
Who is the man that would risk his neck for his broth-er man?

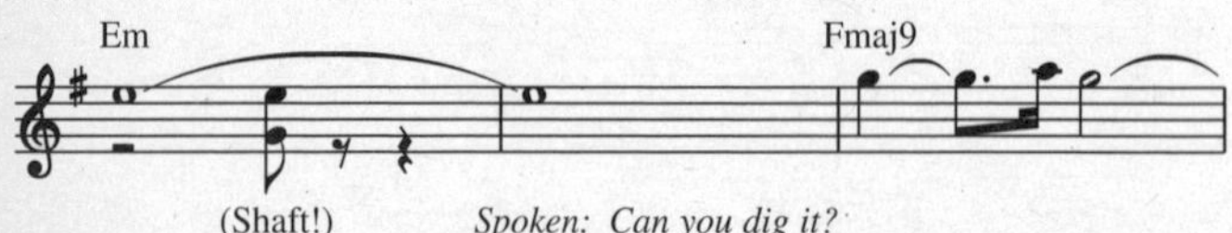
Em
Fmaj9
(Shaft!) Spoken: Can you dig it?

Em
Fmaj9
Sung:
Who's the cat that won't cop-out when there's dan - ger all a - bout?

Em
Fmaj9
(Shaft!) Spoken: Right on! They say this cat Shaft is a

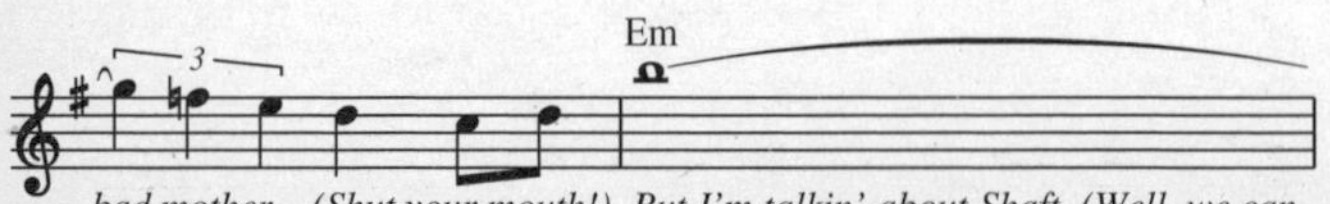
Em
bad mother. (Shut your mouth!) But I'm talkin' about Shaft. (Well, we can

Fmaj9
dig it.)
Sung: He's a com - pli - cat - ed man, but

Em

no one un - der-stands him but his wom - an. *Spoken: John*

G

Shaft!

Fmaj7

N.C.

Fmaj7 N.C.

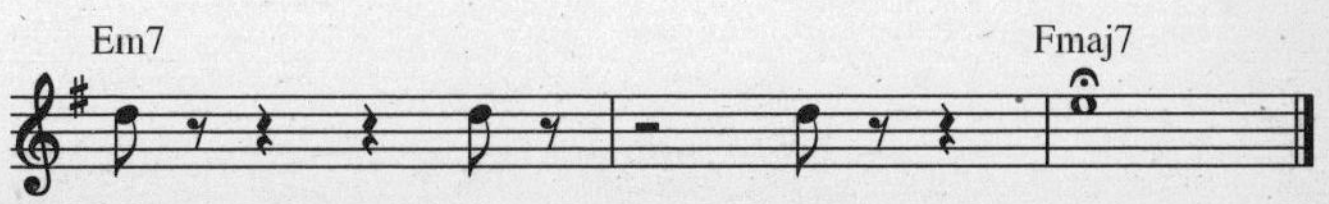
Em7
Fmaj7

(Sittin' On)
THE DOCK OF THE BAY

Words and Music by STEVE CROPPER
and OTIS REDDING

E G6
Ooh, I'm just sit - tin' on the dock of the bay,
To Coda 1
A G E
wast - in' time. I
2
E G D C
Looks like noth-in's gon-na change;
G D C
ev - 'ry-thing still re-mains the same.
G D C
I can't do what ten peo-ple tell me to do,
D.C. al Coda
F D
so I guess I'll re - main the same.
CODA
E G
(Instrumental)
Repeat ad lib.
E

634-5789

Words and Music by EDDIE FLOYD
and STEVE CROPPER

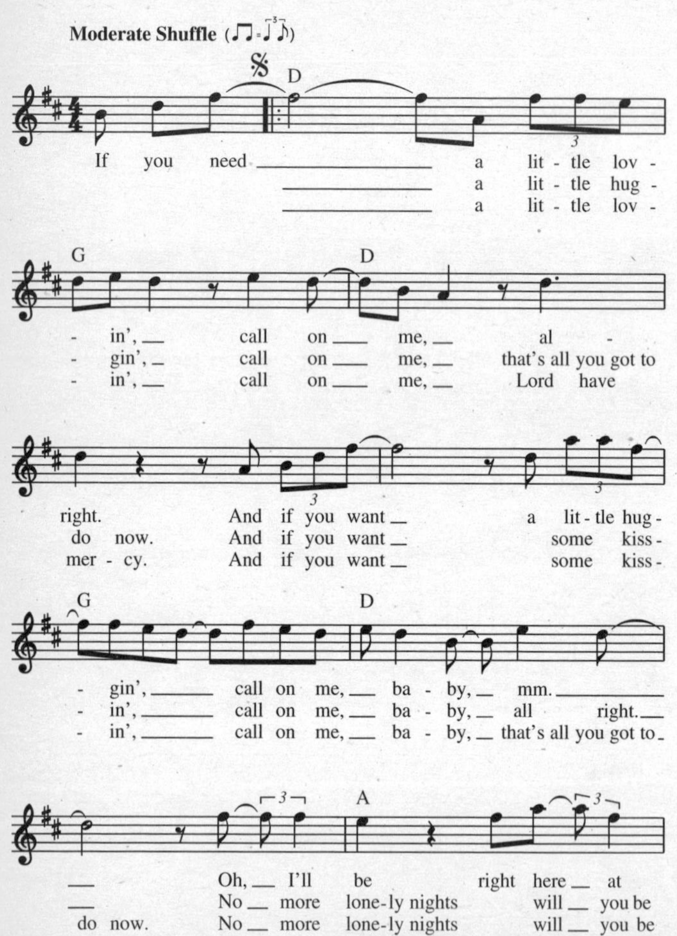
Moderate Shuffle
D
G
D
If you need a lit - tle lov - in', call on me, al - right.
a lit - tle hug - gin', call on me, that's all you got to do now.
a lit - tle lov - in', call on me, Lord have mer - cy.
And if you want a lit - tle hug - gin', call on me, ba - by, mm.
And if you want some kiss - in', call on me, ba - by, all right.
And if you want some kiss - in', call on me, ba - by, that's all you got to do now.
A
Oh, I'll be right here at
No more lone-ly nights will you be
No more lone-ly nights will you be

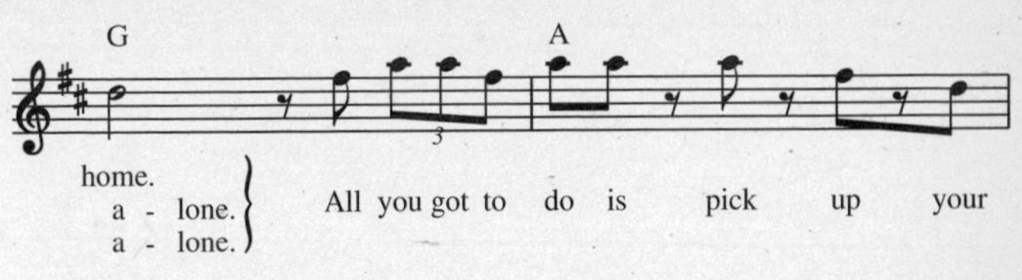
G
A
home.
a - lone.
a - lone.
All you got to do is pick up your

G
D Em D Em
tel - e - phone and dial now, (six - three four - five -

To Coda
D Em D Em D Em D Em
sev - en - eight - nine,) What's my num - ber?
(six - three - four - five -

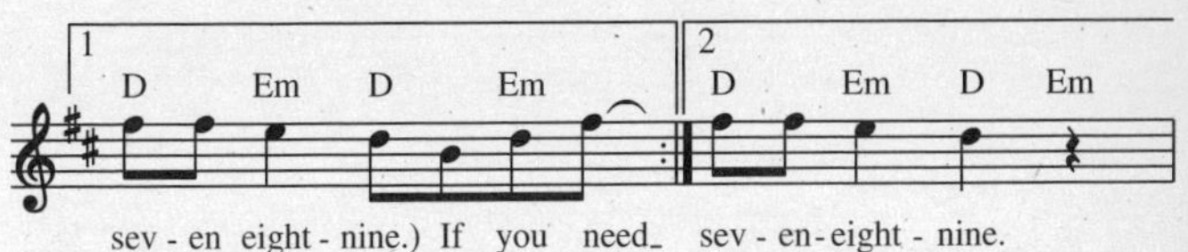
1
2
D Em D Em D Em D Em
sev - en eight - nine.) If you need sev - en - eight - nine.

Bm
Oh, I'll be right there,

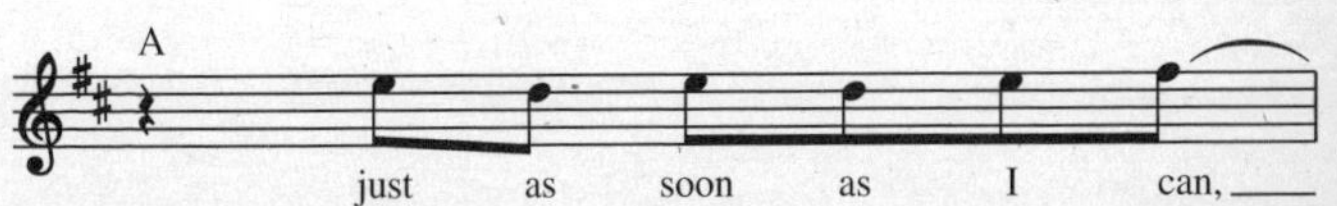
A
just as soon as I can,

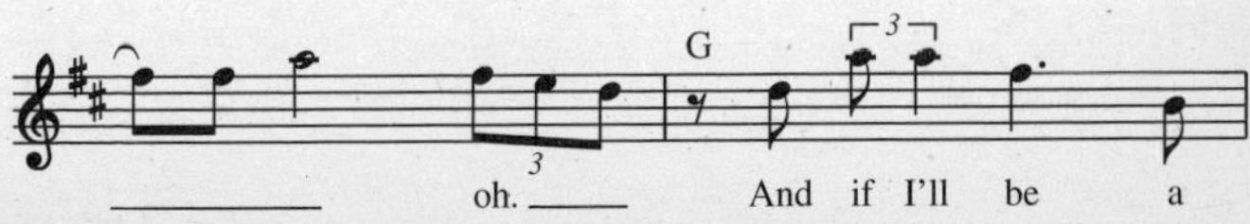
G
oh. And if I'll be a

lit - tle bit late now, I

A
hope that you'll un - der - stand, whoa,

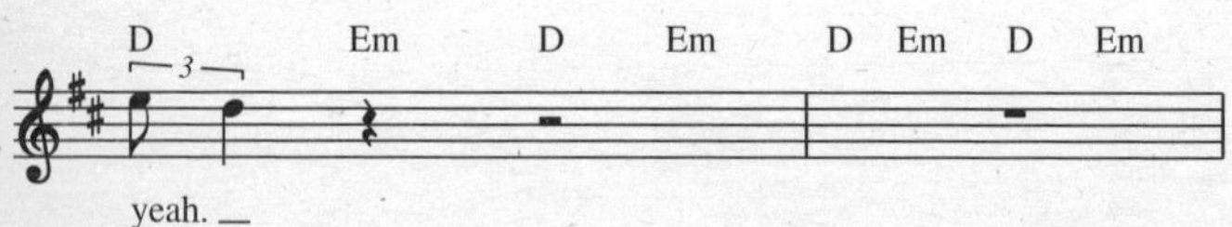
D Em D Em D Em D Em
yeah.

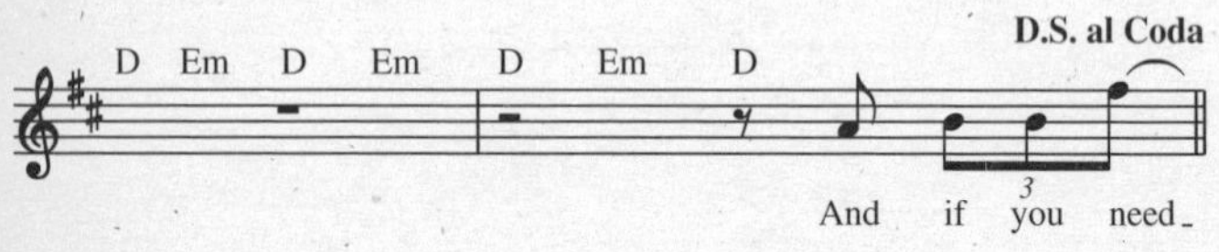
D.S. al Coda
D Em D Em D Em D
And if you need

CODA

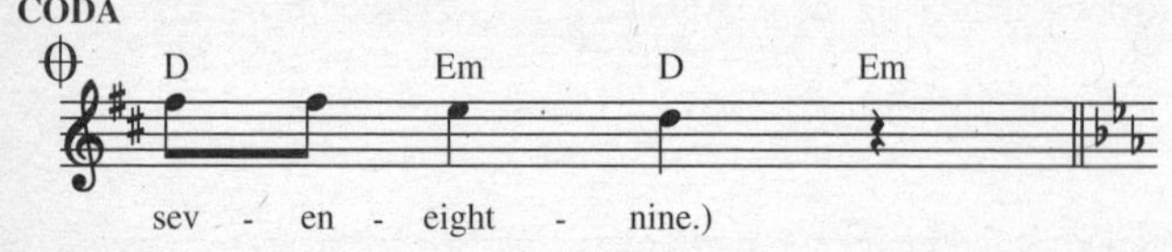
D Em D Em
sev - en - eight - nine.)

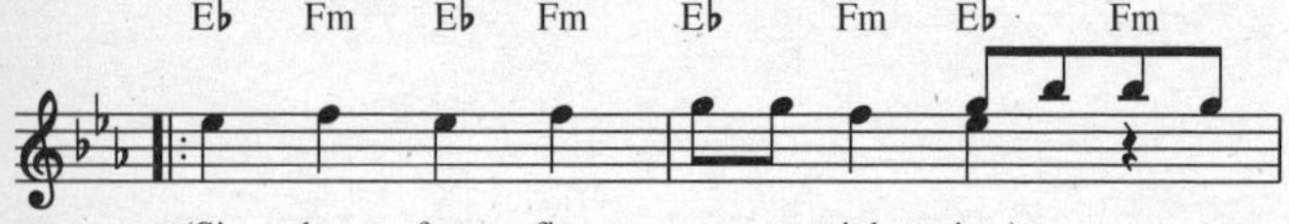
E♭ Fm E♭ Fm E♭ Fm E♭ Fm
(Six - three - four - five - sev - en - eight - nine,)
Call me on the

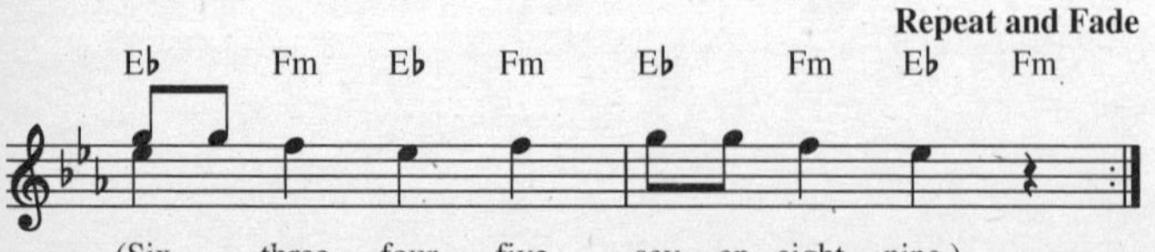
Repeat and Fade
E♭ Fm E♭ Fm E♭ Fm E♭ Fm
(Six - three - four - five - sev - en - eight - nine.)
tel - e - phone.

SON OF SHAFT

Words and Music by ALLEN JONES,
HOMER BANKS and WILLIAM BROWN

Play 3 times
E♭maj7
Oh,
Gm
oh, oh, oh, oh, oh, oh, oh, oh, oh.
I was born and raised on
For-ty-fifth Street. Had the prob-lems of a man at the
age of three. My dad-dy was bad
I've been told, so my fam-i-ly's name I
must up - hold. I love by the clock and
live by the gun. If you ev - er met the fa - ther,

Eb
you've met the sun.
(Instrumental)
1
Gm
2
Yeah,
yeah, yeah.
Eb
Gm
(Instrumental)
Eb
Gm7
Spoken: Check me out.
Eb
Gm
Spoken: I'm the son of Shaft, (now you can believe that)
D.C. and Fade
and I feel so good.

SOUL FINGER

Words and Music by BEN CAULEY, CARL CUNNINGHAM,
JAMES ALEXANDER, JIMMY KING, PHALON JONES
and RONNIE CALDWELL

F♯
F
E
Spoken: Soul fin-ger!
F
N.C.
Soul fin-ger!
Soul fin-ger!
C♯m
F♯
B
F♯m
Play 4 times
B
F♯m
N.C.
B
F♯m
D.S. and Fade
B
F♯m
B
F♯m
B
F♯m

SOUL LIMBO

Words and Music by BOOKER T. JONES, DUCK DUNN, STEVE CROPPER and AL JACKSON, JR.

2
G5
C
F
G
F
C
F
G
F
C
F
G
F
C
F
G
F
C
F
G
F
C
F
G
F

C
F
G
F
C
F
G
F
C
F
G
F
1
C
F
G
F
2
C
F
G
F
C
F
G
F
C
F
G
F
C
F
G
F
Repeat and Fade
C
F
G
F

SOUL MAN

Words and Music by ISAAC HAYES
and DAVID PORTER

I'm com - in'.
noth - ing yet.
I can't stop.
I'm a soul man,

F
(Instrumental)
I'm a

G
soul man.
(Instrumental)

I'm a soul man,

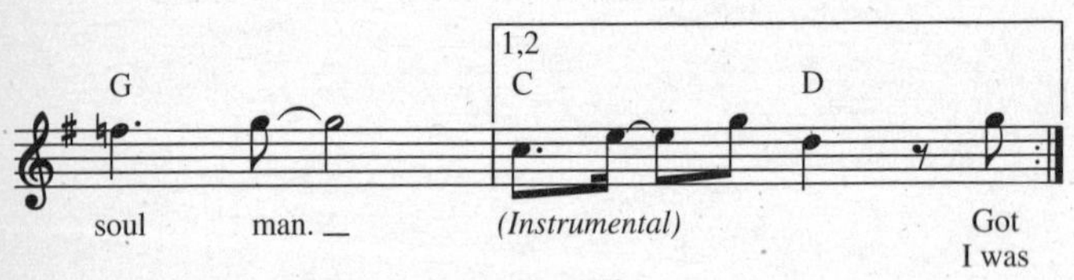

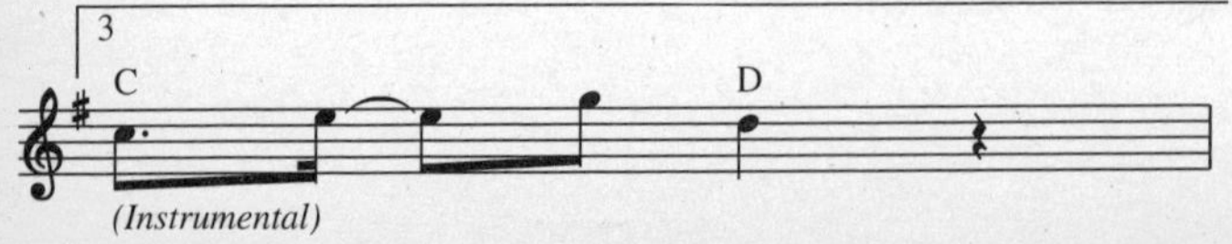

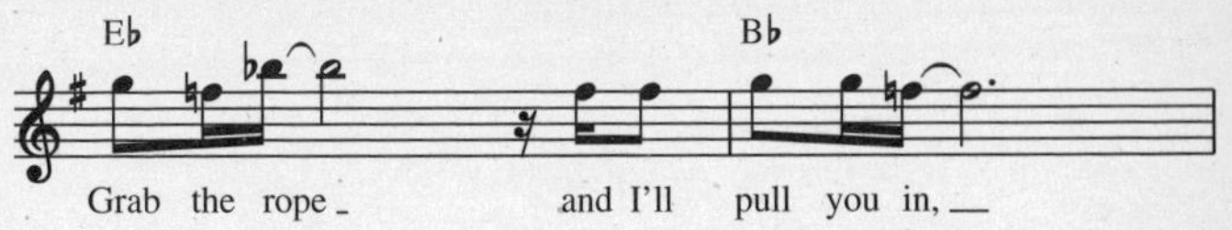
E♭
B♭
Grab the rope
and I'll pull you in,

C
Dsus
give you hope,
and be your on - ly boy - friend,

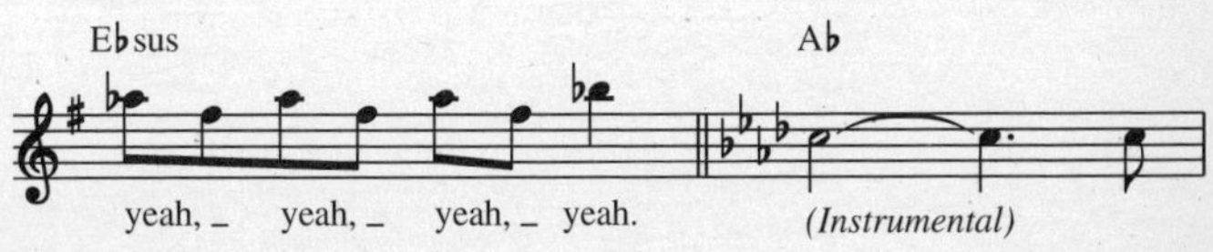
E♭sus
A♭
yeah, yeah, yeah, yeah.
(Instrumental)

G♭
C♭
D♭
E♭
Talk - in' a - bout a
A♭
soul man, I'm a soul man.

Repeat and Fade
Soul man; soul man; I'm a

STAND BY ME

featured in the Motion Picture STAND BY ME

Words and Music by BEN E. KING,
JERRY LEIBER and MIKE STOLLER

dar - ling, dar - ling stand by me,
Dm
C
Dm
stand by me, oh
B♭
C
stand, stand by me,
F
1
stand by me. If the
2
F
Dar - ling stand by me,
Dm
C
Dm
stand by me, oh
B♭
C
stand, stand by me,
F
Repeat and Fade
stand by me. When - ev - er I'm in trou - ble won't you

SUPERSTITION

Words and Music by
STEVIE WONDER

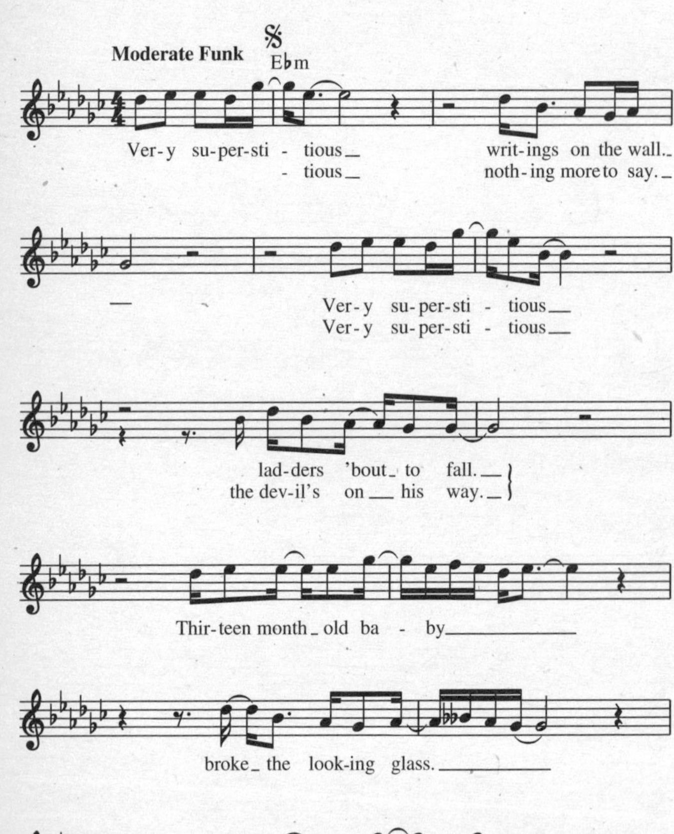

the good things in your past.

B♭
C♭7
When you be - lieve in things that you don't

B♭
A7♭5
A♭
un - der - stand then you suf - fer.

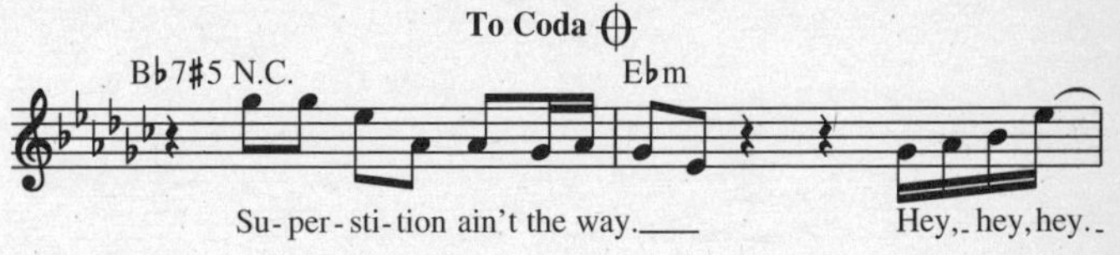
To Coda
B♭7♯5 N.C.
E♭m
Su - per - sti - tion ain't the way.
Hey, hey, hey.

Ooh, ver - y su - per - sti -

- tious.
Wash your face and hands.

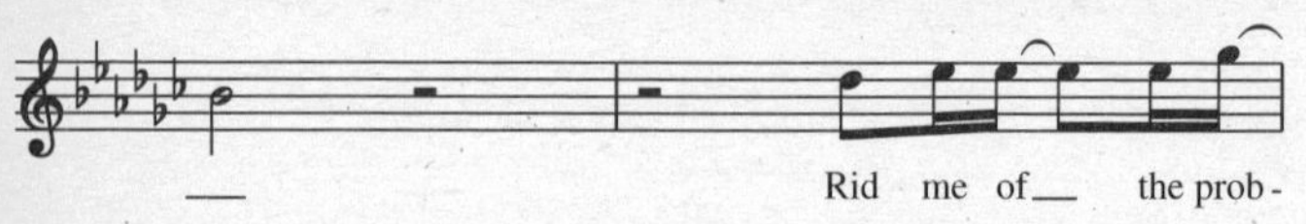
Rid me of the prob -

3
- lems,
do all that you

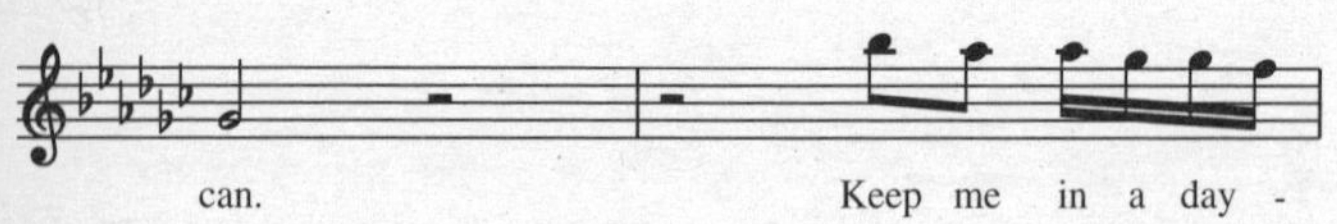
can.
Keep me in a day -

- dream,
3
keep me go-in' strong.

You don't wan - na save

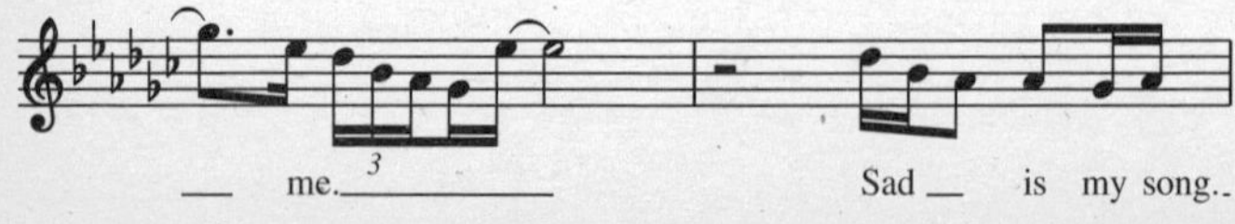
me.
3
Sad is my song.

When you be - lieve

B♭
C♭7
B♭
A7♭5
in things you don't un - der - stand then you suf -

A♭
- fer.

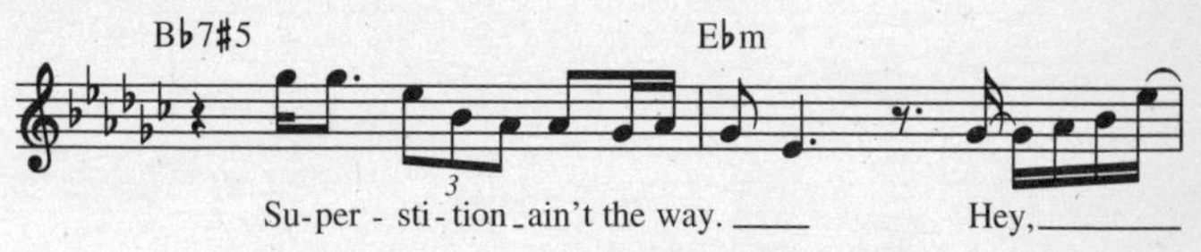
B♭7♯5
E♭m
3
Su-per - sti-tion ain't the way.
Hey,

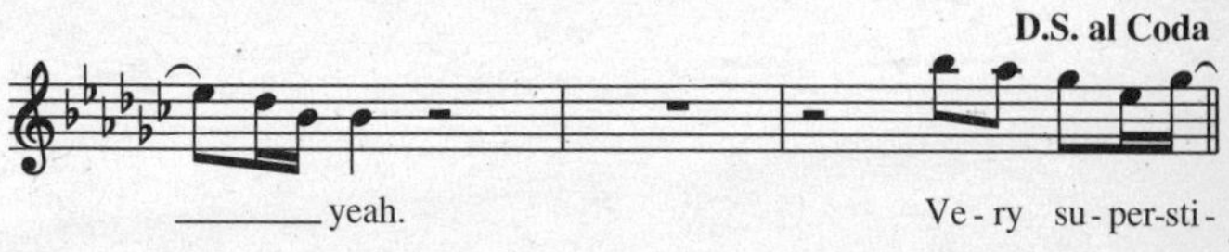
D.S. al Coda
yeah.
Ve - ry su - per-sti -

CODA
E♭m
Repeat and Fade

TAKE ME TO THE RIVER

Words and Music by AL GREEN
and MABON HODGES

A7
in love to stay?
in love to stay?
(Take me, take me.) Take me to the
(Instrumental)
E7
D A
riv - er, and wash me down.
E7
D A
Won't you cleanse my soul,
E7
Dsus A
get my feet on the
To Coda
1
2
To Next Strain
E7
D A
ground?
(Instrumental ends)
3
D.C. al Coda
D A
C♯m
Hold me,
A7
C♯m
love me, squeeze me,

A7
G/D
tease me till I die,
B7
till I die.
Take me,
D.S.
(Take 3rd ending)
CODA
ba-by, take me to the
D A
Yeah, yeah,
E7
D A
yeah, yeah,
E7
D A
yeah.
Dip me in the
E7
D A
wa - ter, dip me in the
E7
1,2
D A
wa - ter, ba - by.
Dip me in the
3
D A
E7

THERE GOES MY BABY

Words and Music by JERRY LEIBER, MIKE STOLLER,
BEN E. NELSON, LOVER PATTERSON and GEORGE TREADWELL

Dm7
G7
C
What can I do?
(There goes my
ba - by.)
Am
(There goes my
ba - by.)
Dm7
(There goes my ba - by.)
G7
Dm7
G7
(There she goes.) Yes, I wan - na know. Did she
C
Am
love me? Did she real - ly love me?
left me. Why did she leave me
3
Dm7
3
Was she just play - ing me for a
so all a - lone, so all a -
1
G7
2
G7
Dm7
fool? I won - der why she lone? I
G7
C
was gon - na tell her that I love her,

Am
and that I need her
be - side my
Dm7
side
to be my guide.
G7
Dm7
G7
C
I wan - na know,
where is my,
Am
where is my ba - by?
Dm7
I want my ba - by,
I need my
G7
Dm7
C
ba - by, yes,
oh,
Am
oh,
G7
F6
C
C6
oh.

THE TEARS OF A CLOWN

Words and Music by STEVIE WONDER,
WILLIAM "SMOKEY" ROBINSON and HENRY COSBY

Moderately bright
D♭ G♭
Now, if there's a smile __ up - on my face _
__ to be care - free, _
D.S. (See additional lyrics)
C♭ G♭ D♭ G♭
__ it's on - ly there _ try - ing to fool _ the pub -
__ it's on - ly to cam - ou - flage ___ my sad -
C♭ G♭ D♭ G♭
- lic; but when it comes _ down to fool - ing you, _
- ness in or - der to shield _ my ___ pride I try _
C♭ G♭ D♭ G♭
__ now hon - ey that's _ quite a dif-f'rent sub -
__ to cov - er this hurt ___ with a show of glad -
C♭ G♭ D♭ G♭
- ject. Don't let my glad ex - pres -
- ness. But don't let my show con - vince _
C♭ G♭ D♭ G♭
- sion give you ______ the wrong im - pres -
__ you that I've ___ been ___ hap - py since _

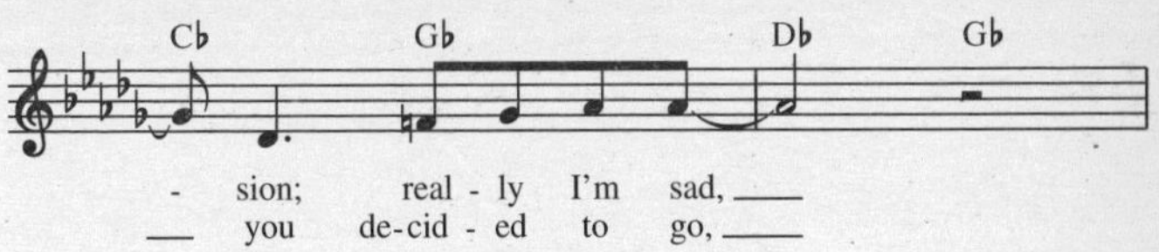
C♭ G♭ D♭ G♭
- sion; real - ly I'm sad,
you de-cid - ed to go,

C♭ G♭ D♭ G♭
oh, sad - der than sad, you're gone
I need you so, I'm hurt

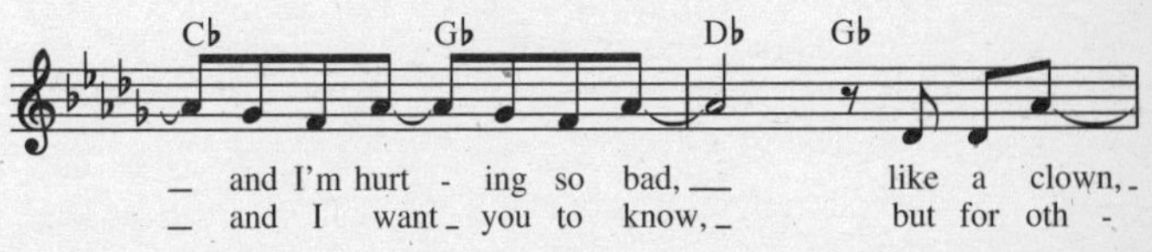
C♭ G♭ D♭ G♭
and I'm hurt - ing so bad, like a clown,
and I want you to know, but for oth -

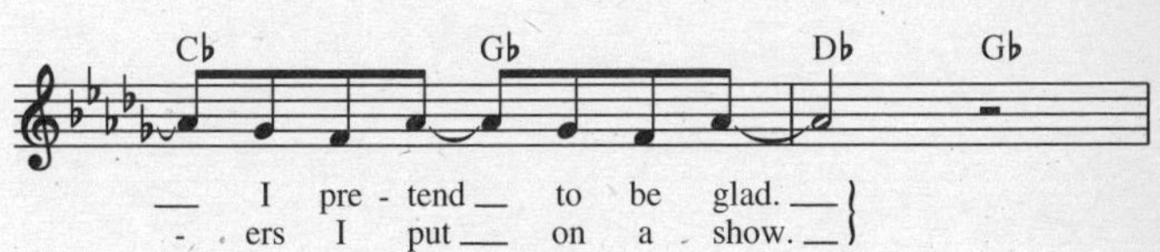
C♭ G♭ D♭ G♭
I pre - tend to be glad.
- ers I put on a show.

C♭ G♭ A♭
Now there's some sad things known to man

F/A B♭m
but ain't too much sad - der than

Gbmaj7
Db N.C.
the tears of a clown,

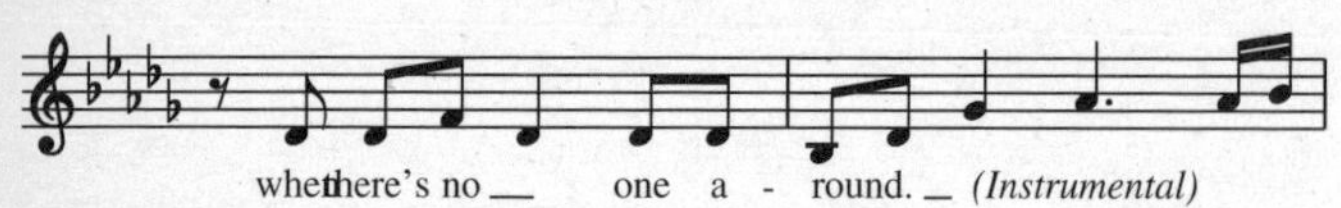
when there's no one a - round. (Instrumental)

1
Db Gb

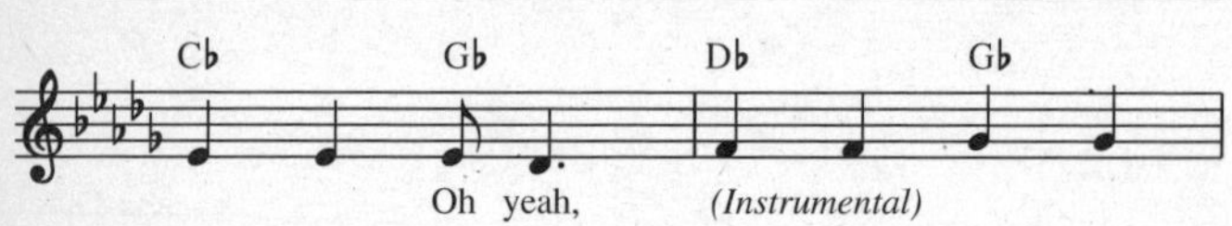
Cb Gb Db Gb
Oh yeah, (Instrumental)

Cb Gb
2
Db Gb
Now, if I ap - pear Just like Pag - li -

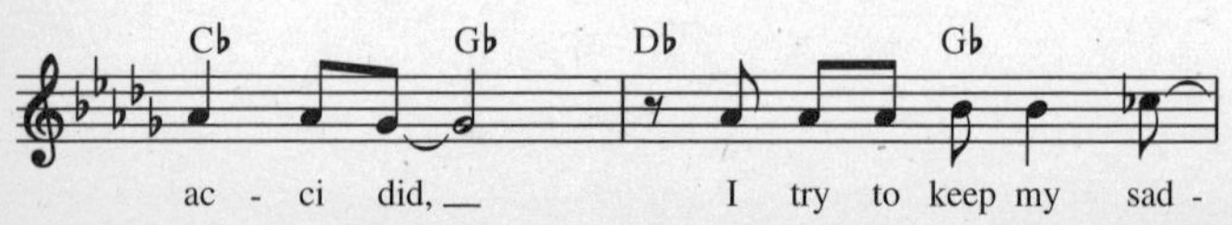
Cb Gb Db Gb
ac - ci did, I try to keep my sad -

Cb Gb Db Gb
- ness hid, smil - ing in the pub - lic eye

Cb Gb Db Gb
but in my lone - ly room I cry

Cb Gb Db
the tears of a clown,

Gb Cb Gb
when there's no one a-round. Oh yeah,

D.S. and Fade
Db Gb Cb Gb
ba - by! Now, if there's a smile

Additional Lyrics

Now, if there's a smile on my face
Don't let my glad expression
Give you a wrong impression
Don't let this smile I wear
Make you think that I don't care *(Fade)*

TELL IT LIKE IT IS

Words and Music by GEORGE DAVIS
and LEE DIAMOND

Slow 4
Gm
If you want some-thing to
C7
F
Fmaj7
play with go and find your-self a toy.
F6
D7
Gm
Ba-by my time is too ex-pen-sive,
C7
F
Fmaj7
and I'm not a lit-tle boy.
F6
F
Am
Dm
If you are se-ri-ous,
Am
Dm
don't play with my heart it makes me fu-ri-ous.
Am
B♭
But if you want me to love you ba-by I

C7
Gm7
C7
will, girl, you know I will. Tell it like it
Gm
C7
Gm7
C9
is, don't be a - shamed, let your con-science be your
F
Fmaj7
F6
D7
guide. But I know deep down in -
Gm
C7
Gm7
C9
side of me I be-lieve you love me, for - get your fool-ish
F
Fmaj7
F6
F
pride.
Am
Dm
Life is too short to have sor - row
Am
Dm
you may be here to - day and gone to - mor - row.
Am
B♭
You might as well get what you want so go on and
D.S. and Fade
C7
Gm7
C7
live, ba - by go on and live. Tell it like it

THESE ARMS OF MINE

Words and Music by
OTIS REDDING

Moderately slow
Bb
These arms of mine, they are
F7
Eb
lone - ly, lone - ly and feel - ing
Bb
blue. These arms of mine, they are
F7
Eb
yearn-ing, yearn - ing from want - ing
Bb
Bb+
you. And if you would let them
Bb6
Bb7
Eb
F7
hold you, oh I'll grieve for,
Bb
I be - lieve. These arms of

F7
mine, they are burn - ing,
Eb
Bb
burn - ing for want-ing you. These arms of
F7
mine, they are long - ing,
Eb
Bb
long - ing to hold you. And if you
Bb+
Bb6
Bb7
would let them hold you,
Eb
F7
Bb
oh I'll grieve for, I be - lieve.
Repeat and Fade
Eb
F
Bb
Bb7

Vocal ad lib. (See additional lyrics)

Additional Lyrics

Come home, baby,
Just be my little woman,
Just be my lovin'
Oh, I need somebody
Oh, to treat me right,
Oh, I need two warm lovin' arms to hold me tight.
And I need your tender lips to hold me,
Oh, hold me tight.

THINK

Words and Music by
LOWMAN PAULING

D7
To Coda
A7
one who loves you.
Think a - bout the
How much of all your
D7
sac - ri - fic - es
hap - pi - ness,
that I made
can I real -
for you.
ly claim?
Think a - bout the
How man - y tears have
hard times
you shed
that I spent
for which I was
for you.
to blame?
Think a - bout the
I don't re -
A7
good things
mem - ber
that I've done for you.
what they bought.
Think a - bout the
I tried so hard to

bad things I've tried
please you, at least that's
1
not to do. Come on chil - dren and
what I thought.
2
D.C. al Coda
CODA
A7
Come on chil - dren and
La - dy be - fore you leave me,
G7
re - al - ize that I'm the
D7
1
A7
one who loves you.
2
A7
D7

THE THRILL IS GONE

Words and Music by ROY HAWKINS
and RICK DARNELL

Slow Blues tempo
Bm
1. The thrill is gone, _ The thrill is gone _ a -
2.-4. (See additional lyrics)
way.
B7
Em
The thrill is gone ___ ba - by,
Bm
The thrill is gone ___ a - way. _
Gmaj7
F#7
You know you done me wrong ___ ba - by, _ and you'll be sor -
Em
Bm
1-3
F#7
4
F#7
- ry some day. ___

Additional Lyrics

2. The thrill is gone, it's gone away from me. *(2 times)*
Although I'll still live on, but so lonely I'll be.

3. The thrill is gone, it's gone away for good. *(2 times)*
Someday I know I'll be over it all, baby, just like I know a good man should.

4. You know I'm free, free now, baby, I'm free from your spell. *(2 times)*
And now that it's all over, all I can do is wish you well.

TIME IS TIGHT

Words and Music by BOOKER T. JONES, DUCK DUNN,
STEVE CROPPER and AL JACKSON, JR.

G7
C
F
C
F
To Coda
C
1
2
F

C
CODA
D.S. al Coda
C
Repeat and Fade

TOUCH A HAND, MAKE A FRIEND

Words and Music by CARL HAMPTON, HOMER BANKS and RAYMOND JACKSON

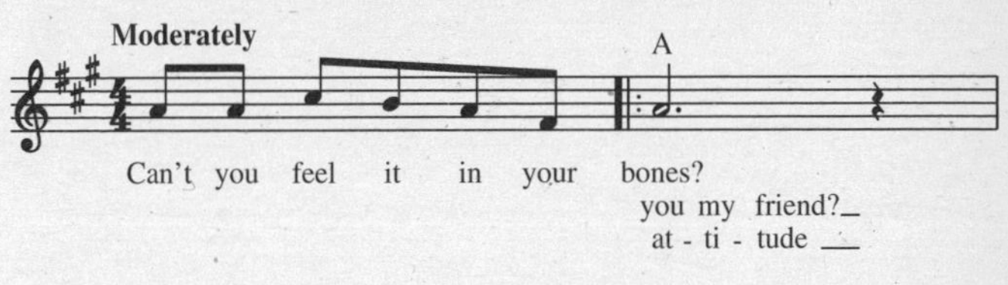
Moderately
A
Can't you feel it in your bones?
you my friend?
at - ti - tude

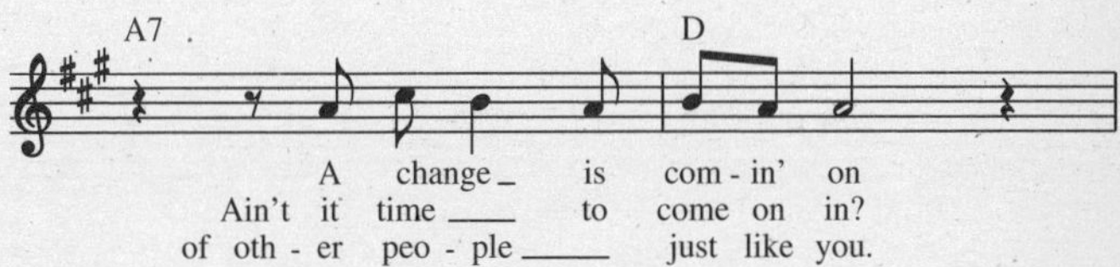
A7
D
A change is com - in' on
Ain't it time to come on in?
of oth - er peo - ple just like you.

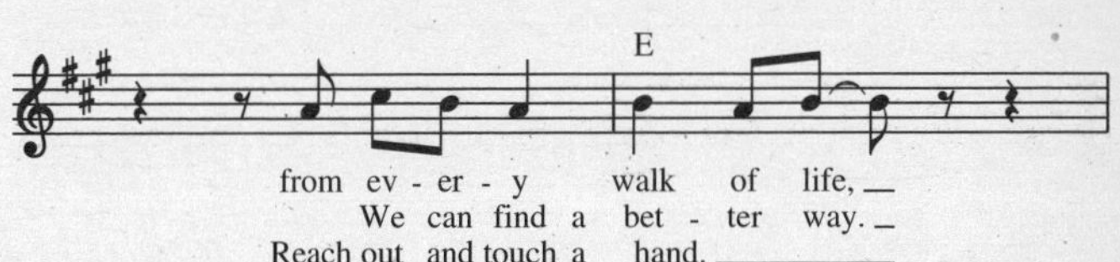
E
from ev - er - y walk of life,
We can find a bet - ter way.
Reach out and touch a hand.

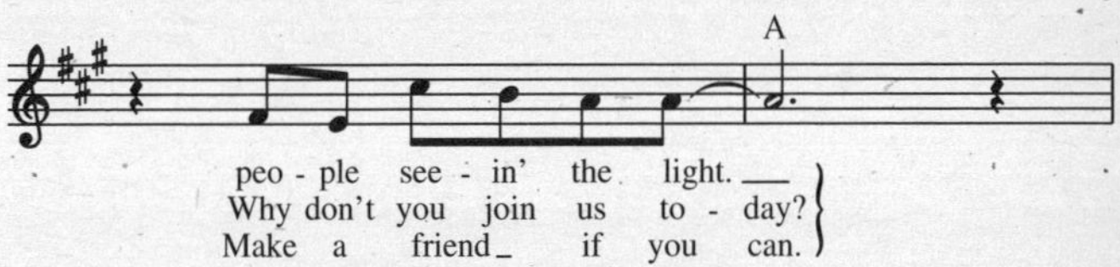
A
peo - ple see - in' the light.
Why don't you join us to - day?
Make a friend if you can.

Can't you feel it in your heart now?

A7
D
A new thing is tak - in' shape;

E
reach out and touch a hand,

A
make a friend if you can.

Reach out and touch a hand,

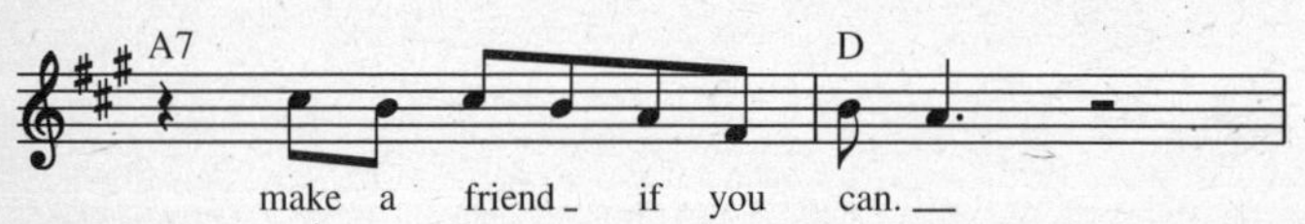
A7
D
make a friend if you can.

E
Reach out and touch a hand,

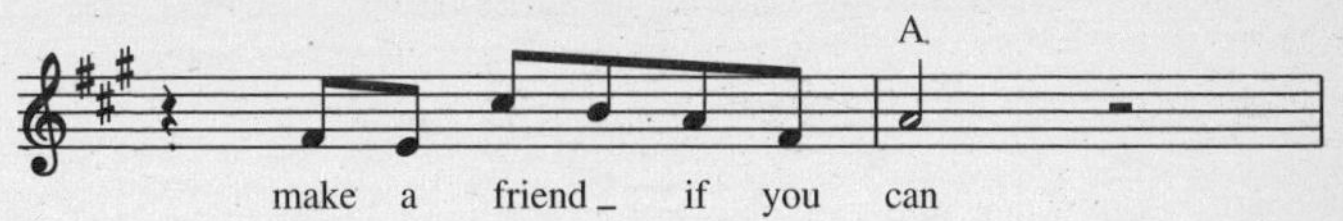
A
make a friend _ if you can

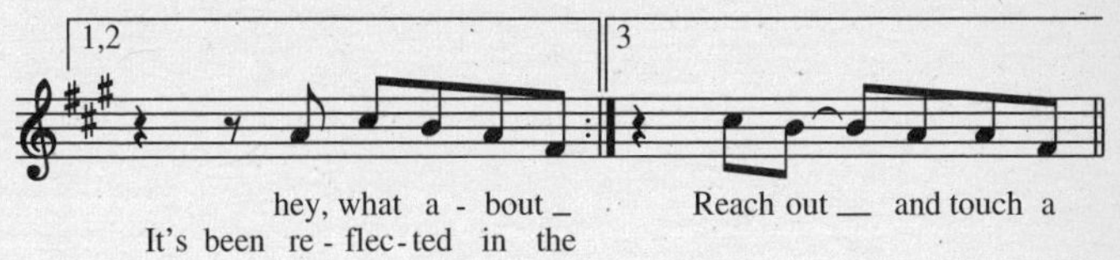
1,2
3
hey, what a - bout _
It's been re - flec-ted in the
Reach out _ and touch a

A7
hand,
make a friend _ if you

D
can. _
Reach out _ and touch a

E
hand,
make a friend _ if you

Repeat and Fade
A
can.
Reach out _ and touch a

TIRED OF BEING ALONE

Words and Music by
AL GREEN

Moderately
C
I'm so tired of being alone, I'm so tired
Cmaj7
of on my own, won't you
C7
help me, girl, just as soon
Am
as you can?
A7
D
People say that I
I guess you know that I
Dmaj7
3
D7
found a way to make you say that you
love you so even though you don't

Bm7
B7
love me.
want me no more.
G
A
F♯
G
A
G
You did - n't go for that,
it's a nat - 'ral fact,
Now I'm cry - in' tears,
all through the years,
A
F♯
that I wan - na come back;
I'll tell you like it is;
G7
1
show me where it's at.
Ba - by.
love me if you will.
2
I'm so tired
D
Dmaj7
(Instrumental)
Repeat and Fade
D7
Bm

WALKIN' THE DOG

Words and Music by
RUFUS THOMAS

N.C./E
1
2
Em7
Mar - y, Mar - y, quite ___ con - trar - y,
how does your gar - den grow? _ (Ver-y well.)
Sil - ver bells and lit-tle bit-ty bit-ty bob-tails;
E5 N.C.
pret-ty maids all in a row. ___ Walk-in' your dog._
A
I'm just a - walk - in' your
E
dog. _ (Whoa _ whoa ___ whoa whoa whoa

whoa.)
Well, if you
B
don't know how to do it, I'll
A
show ya how to walk the dog.
3
N.C./E
Well, if you
B
don't know how to do it, I'll
A
N.C./E
show ya how to walk the dog.
B
Well, if you don't how how to do it, I'll
A
Em7
show ya how to walk the dog.

WHERE DID OUR LOVE GO

Words and Music by BRIAN HOLLAND,
LAMONT DOZIER and EDWARD HOLLAND

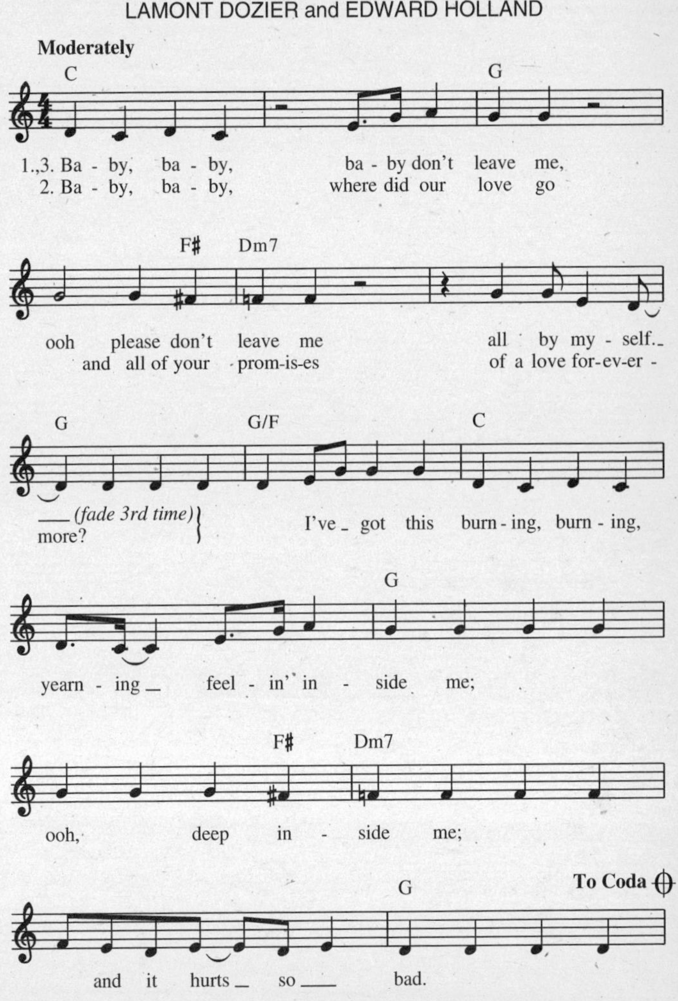

G/F
C
You came in - to my heart (ba - by ba - by)
ren-der (ba - by ba - by)
G
3
so tell me with a burn-ing love
so help me sweet you now want to
Dm
1
(ba - by ba - by) that stings like a
leave. (ba - by ba - by)
G
bee. (ba - by ba - by) Now that I sur -
2
Dm7
G
Ooh, you wan - na leave me (ba - by ba - by)
G/F
C
ooh. (ba - by ba - by) Ba - by ba - by
(Instrumental)
G
F♯
where did our love go? Ooh, don't you

Dm7
want me;
(ba - by ba - by)
Don't you want me no
G
more ba - by, ba - by?
1
G/F
Ooh, ba - by.
2
G/F
D.C. al Coda
CODA
G/F
Be - fore you won my
C
heart (ba - by ba - by)
you were a per - fect
G
guy;
but now that you
Dm7
got me
(ba - by ba - by)
you wan - na leave me be -
G
D.C. and Fade
hind ba - by, ba - by,
ooh ba - by.
(ba - by ba - by)

WHAT'D I SAY

Words and Music by
RAY CHARLES

Medium Bounce

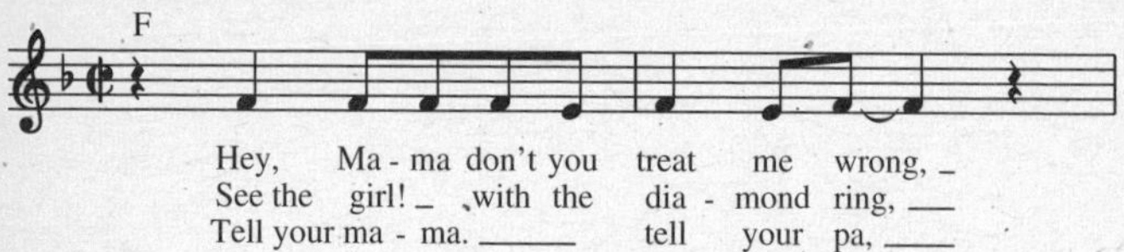
F
Hey, Ma - ma don't you treat me wrong,
See the girl! with the dia - mond ring,
Tell your ma - ma. tell your pa,

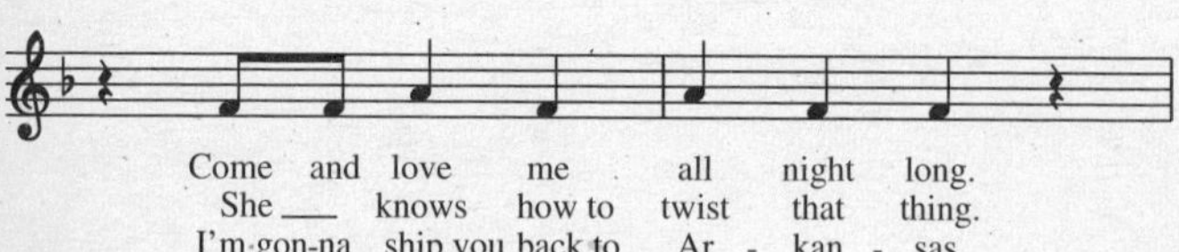
Come and love me all night long.
She knows how to twist that thing.
I'm gon-na ship you back to Ar - kan - sas.

B♭9
B♭7
F7
Oh, oh, hey, hey,
Oh, oh, hey, hey,
Oh, yes, You don't do right,

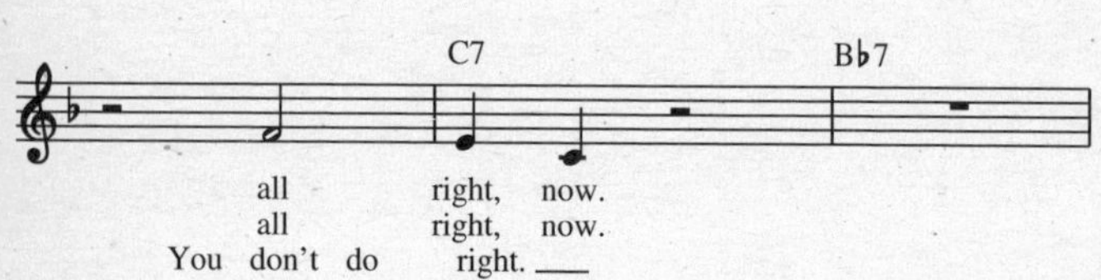
C7
B♭7
all right, now.
all right, now.
You don't do right.

F7
1,2
3
F
Tell me what'd I

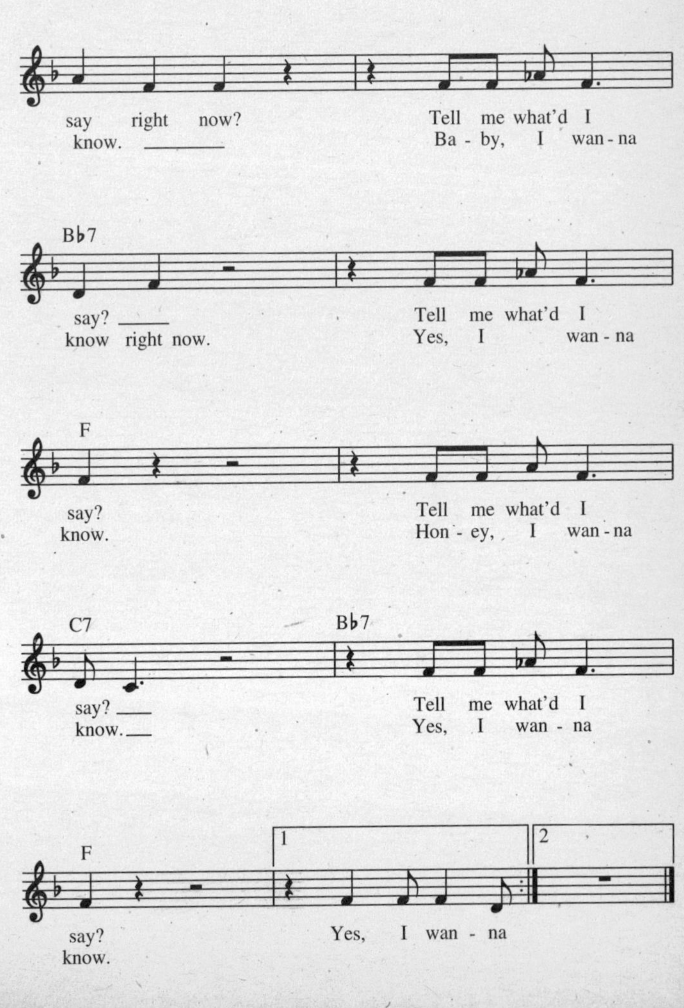
say?
know.
Tell me what'd I
I wan - na
say right now?
know.
Tell me what'd I
Ba - by, I wan - na
B♭7
say?
know right now.
Tell me what'd I
Yes, I wan - na
F
say?
know.
Tell me what'd I
Hon - ey, I wan - na
C7
B♭7
say?
know.
Tell me what'd I
Yes, I wan - na
F
1
2
say?
know.
Yes, I wan - na

WRAP IT UP

Words and Music by ISAAC HAYES
and DAVID PORTER

Moderately fast
E♭5
I've been watch-in' you for days now, ba - by.

I just love your sex - y ways now, ba - by. You know

my love will nev - er stop now, ba - by. Just

put your lov - in' in my box, ba - by. Wrap it up,

D♭5
G♭
To Coda
I'll take it. Wrap it up, I'll take

A♭
E♭5
it. Now more will I shop a-round,

ba - by. I know I got _ the best thing in town, _

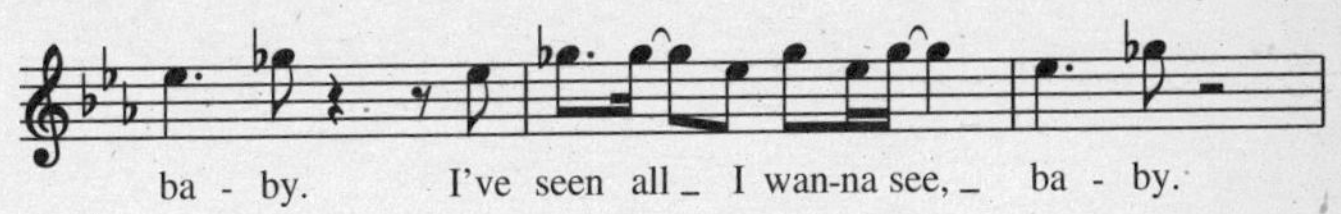
ba - by. I've seen all _ I wan-na see, _ ba - by.

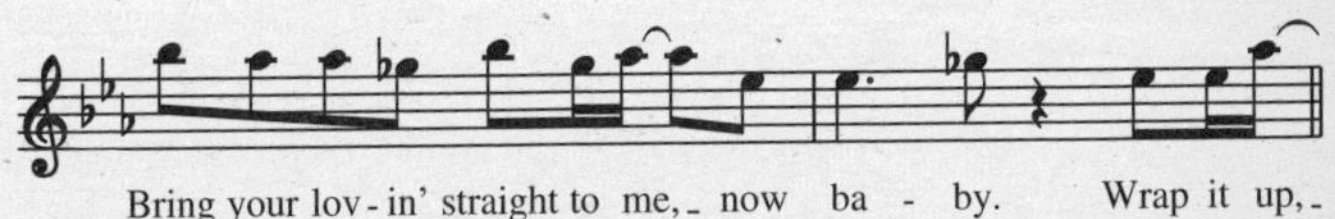
Bring your lov - in' straight to me, _ now ba - by. Wrap it up, _

Eb5
Db5
I'll take ___ it. Wrap it up, _

Gb5
1
Ab5
2
Ab5
I'll take _ it. Wrap it up, _ _ it.

Eb5
Good _ God al-might-y, come on.

Cm
Ooh, ____ I'm gon-na treat you like the queen you are;

bring you sweet things from my can - dy jar, 'cause

you've got treats you ain't nev - er used.

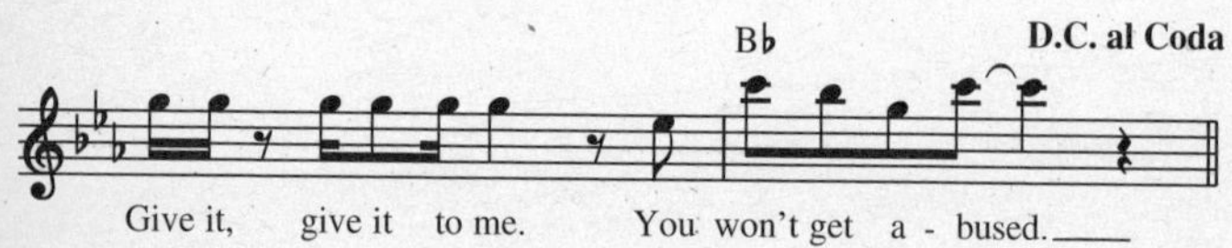
B♭
D.C. al Coda
Give it, give it to me. You won't get a - bused.

CODA
A♭5
E♭5
D♭5
it. Wrap it up, I'll take it. Wrap it up,

G♭5
A♭5
ooh, wrap it up,

E♭5
D♭5
I'll take it. Wrap it up,

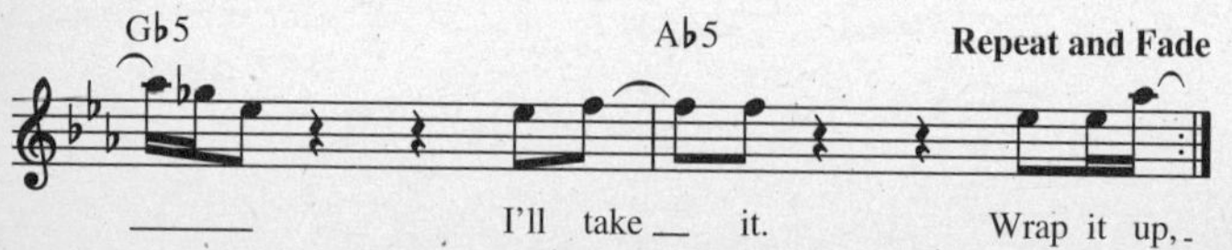
G♭5
A♭5
Repeat and Fade
I'll take it. Wrap it up,

(Your Love Keeps Lifting Me)

HIGHER AND HIGHER

Words and Music by GARY JACKSON,
CARL SMITH and RAYNARD MINER

Em7♭5/D
D
- ed be - fore.
clos - est friend.
So keep it up,
But you came;
Em7/D
quench my de - sire,
he soon de - part - ed,
and I'll be at your side
and he nev - er
Em7♭5/D
D
for - ev - er - more.
showed his face a - gain.
1
2
Now once
I'm so glad
D
I fi - nal - ly found

E/D
you;
you're that "one

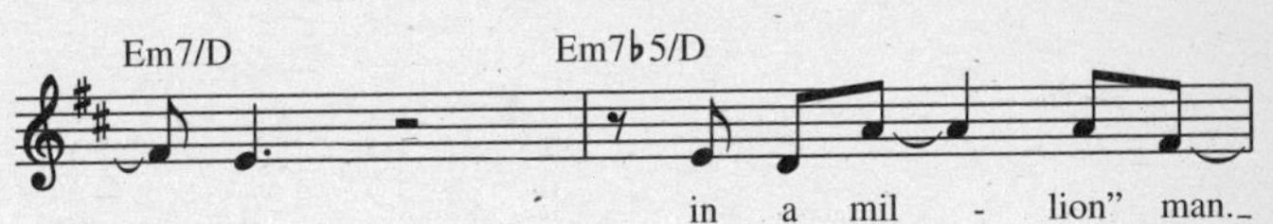
Em7/D
Em7♭5/D
in a mil - lion" man.

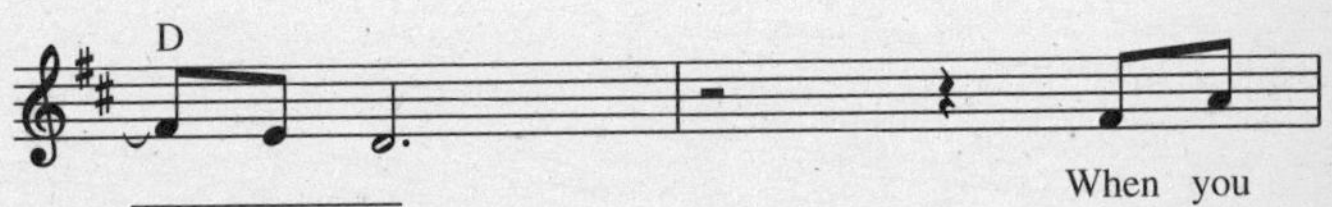
D
When you

wrap
your lov - in' arms a - round

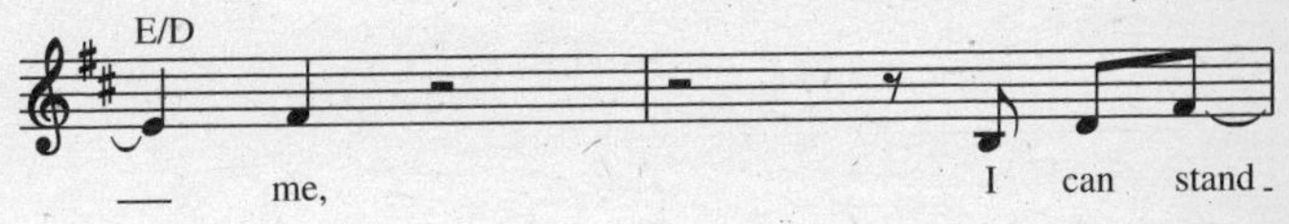
E/D
me,
I can stand

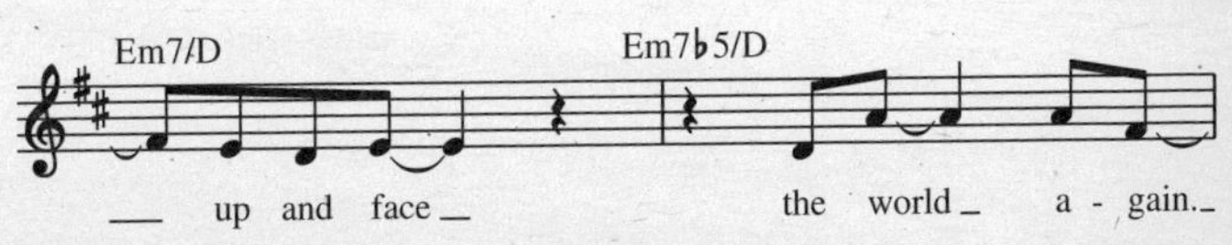
Em7/D
Em7♭5/D
up and face
the world a - gain.

D.S. and Fade

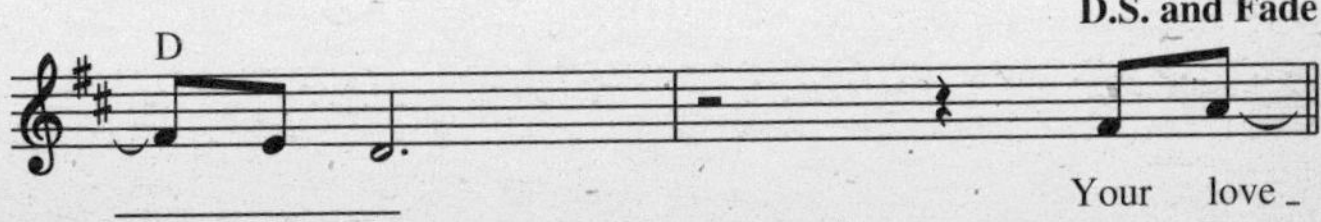
D
Your love

YOU DON'T KNOW LIKE I KNOW

Words and Music by ISAAC HAYES
and DAVID PORTER

Bb
go to her ___ and like a mir - a - cle, ev - 'ry -

Bb7
thing just is al - right. ___

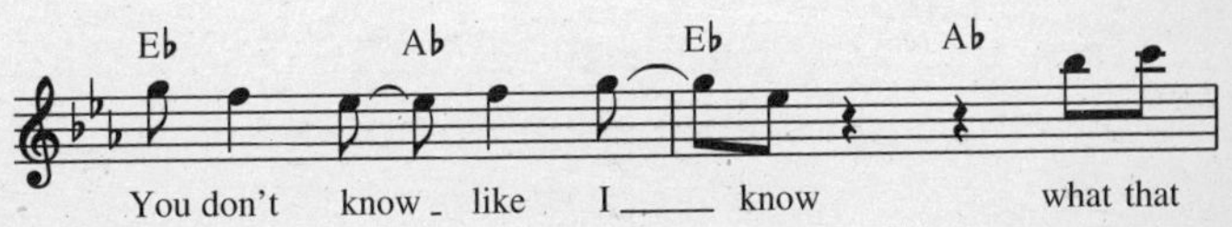
Eb Ab Eb Ab
You don't know _ like I ___ know what that

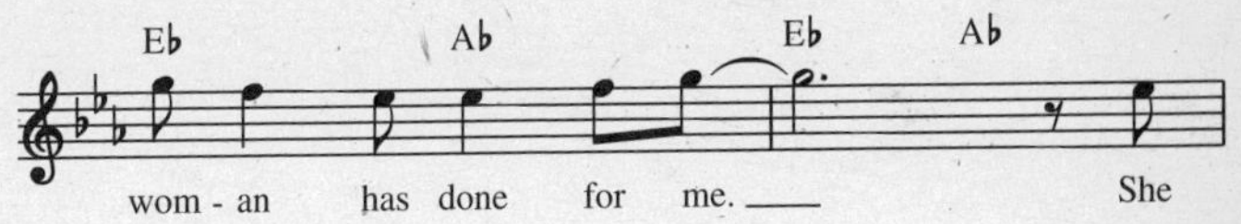
Eb Ab Eb Ab
wom - an has done for me. ___ She

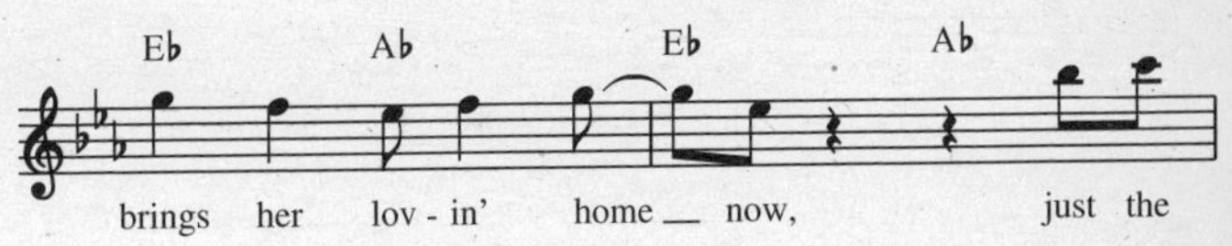
Eb Ab Eb Ab
brings her lov - in' home ___ now, just the

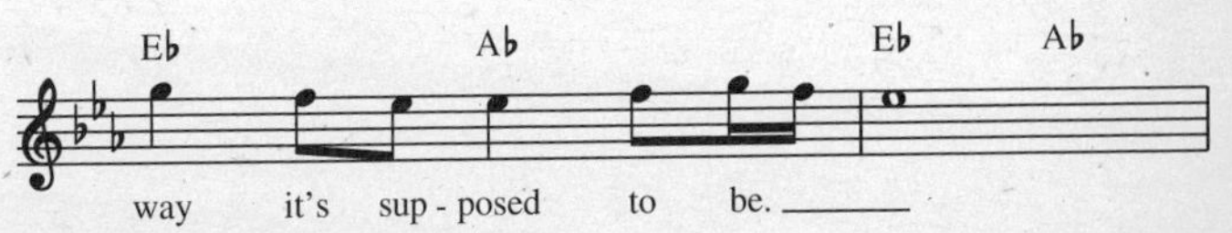
Eb Ab Eb Ab
way it's sup - posed to be. ___

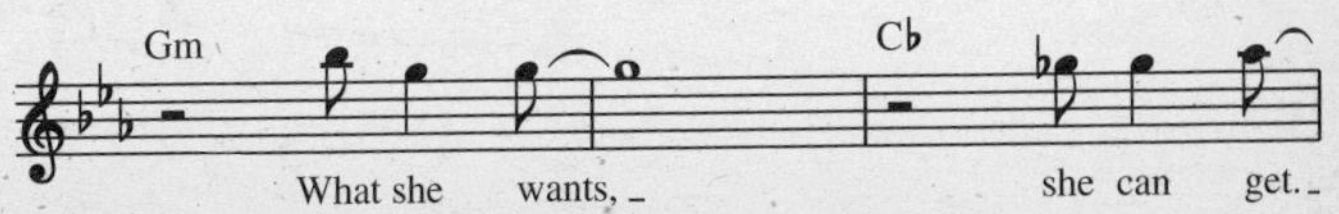
Gm Cb
What she wants, _ she can get. _

B♭
Too much lov - in'.

B♭7
Is she read - y,
is she read - y,

is she read - y to quit?

E♭
(Instrumental)

E♭7
F

G♭

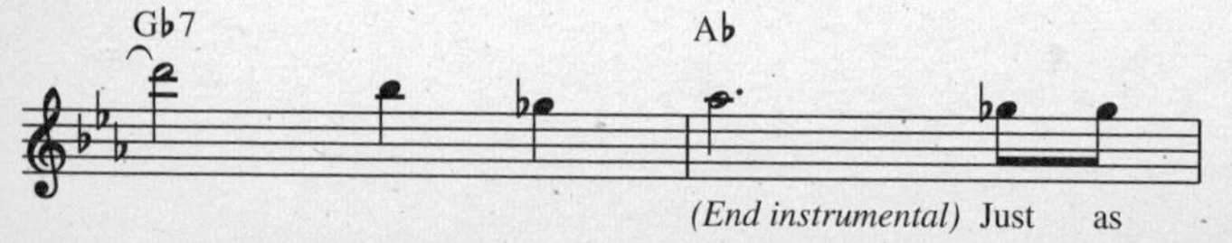
G♭7
A♭
(End instrumental) Just as

Gm
long as I live, yeah, when -
C♭
ev - er trou - ble rise, I
B♭
go to her, and like a mir - a - cle ev - 'ry -
B♭7
D.C. al Coda
CODA
E♭
thing is just al - right.
B♭7
No - bod - y knows, no - bod - y knows,
no - bod - y knows like I know.
Repeat and Fade
E♭
A♭
E♭
A♭
You don't know, you don't know.

GUITAR CHORD FRAMES

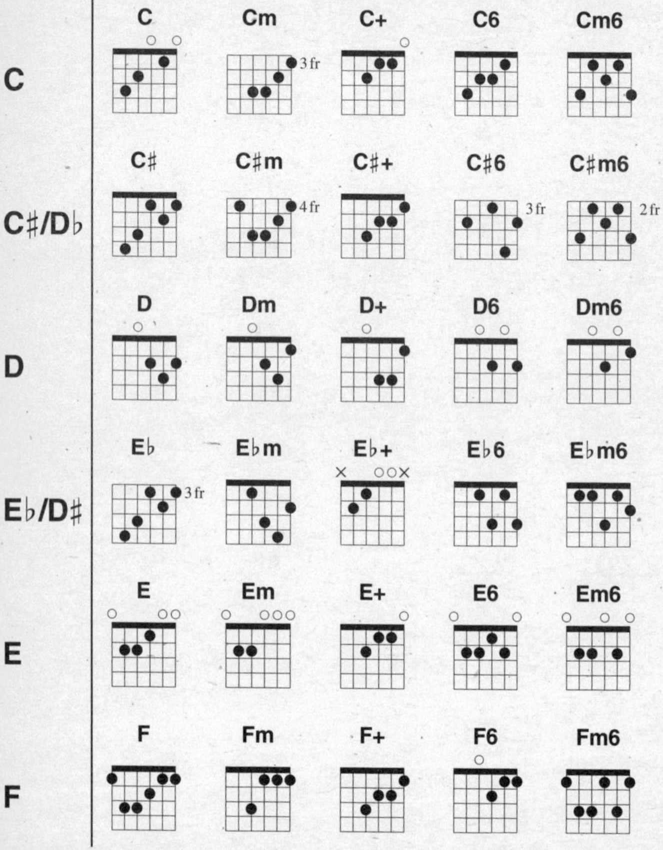

C	C	Cm (3 fr)	C+	C6	Cm6
C♯/D♭	C♯	C♯m (4 fr)	C♯+	C♯6 (3 fr)	C♯m6 (2 fr)
D	D	Dm	D+	D6	Dm6
E♭/D♯	E♭ (3 fr)	E♭m	E♭+	E♭6	E♭m6
E	E	Em	E+	E6	Em6
F	F	Fm	F+	F6	Fm6

This guitar chord reference includes 120 commonly used chords. For a more complete guide to guitar chords, see "THE PAPERBACK CHORD BOOK" (HL00702009).

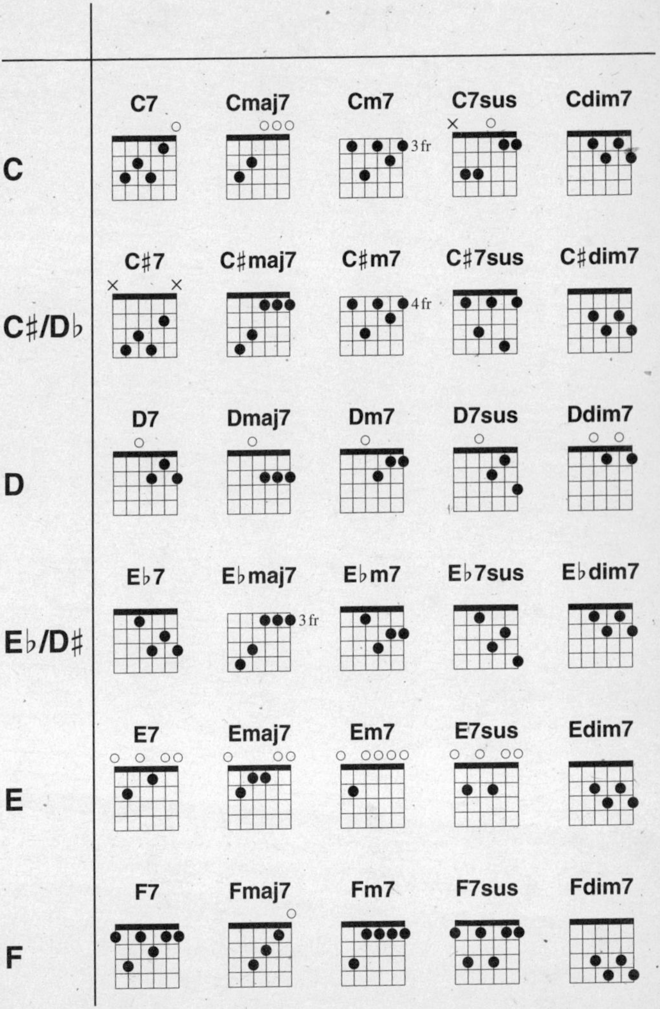

C	C7	Cmaj7	Cm7 (3fr)	C7sus	Cdim7
C♯/D♭	C♯7	C♯maj7	C♯m7 (4fr)	C♯7sus	C♯dim7
D	D7	Dmaj7	Dm7	D7sus	Ddim7
E♭/D♯	E♭7	E♭maj7 (3fr)	E♭m7	E♭7sus	E♭dim7
E	E7	Emaj7	Em7	E7sus	Edim7
F	F7	Fmaj7	Fm7	F7sus	Fdim7

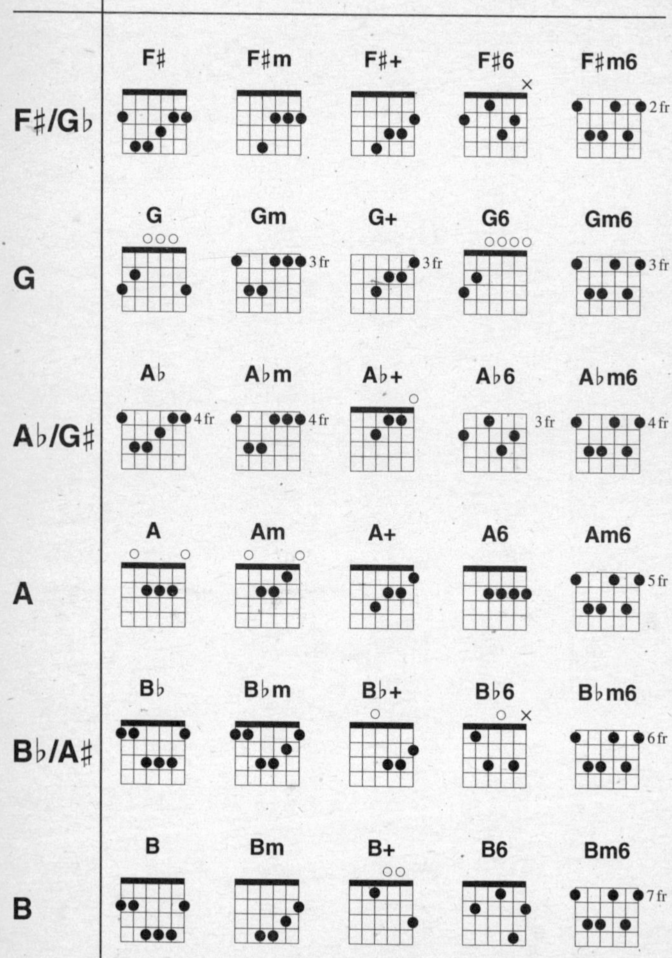
F♯/G♭
F♯
F♯m
F♯+
F♯6
F♯m6
2 fr
G
G
Gm
3 fr
G+
3 fr
G6
Gm6
3 fr
A♭/G♯
A♭
4 fr
A♭m
4 fr
A♭+
A♭6
3 fr
A♭m6
4 fr
A
A
Am
A+
A6
Am6
5 fr
B♭/A♯
B♭
B♭m
B♭+
B♭6
B♭m6
6 fr
B
B
Bm
B+
B6
Bm6
7 fr

F♯/G♭	F♯7	F♯maj7	F♯m7	F♯7sus	F♯dim7
G	G7	Gmaj7	Gm7 (3 fr)	G7sus	Gdim7
A♭/G♯	A♭7 (4 fr)	A♭maj7	A♭m7 (4 fr)	A♭7sus	A♭dim7 (4 fr)
A	A7	Amaj7	Am7	A7sus	Adim7
B♭/A♯	B♭7	B♭maj7	B♭m7	B♭7sus	B♭dim7
B	B7	Bmaj7	Bm7 (2 fr)	B7sus (4 fr)	Bdim7